Forgotten Tales of Utah

Andy Weeks

illustrations by

Sarah Haynes

The History Press

Published by The History Press
Charleston, SC
www.historypress.net

First published 2017

Manufactured in the United States

ISBN 9781467137300

Library of Congress Control Number: 2017934955

In memory of my dad, Floyd V. Weeks.

I hope you're pleased with my efforts. I miss you!

Contents

Contents

Acknowledgements

As this work goes to press, I want to say thanks to the usual cast of characters. Without being cumbersome, I'd like to mention just a few of them here.

As always, I appreciate the encouragement of my wife, Heidi. She's my shining star, and I appreciate the light she's offered me as I've tried to juggle multiple deadlines and projects. Many thanks to my son, Brayden, for his quiet example and encouraging words about my writing projects. I am doubly excited about his accomplishments.

I have nothing but good things to say about my acquisitions editor, Artie Crisp, who has been a pleasure to work with on this book, as have others at Arcadia Publishing and The History Press, including production editor Ryan Finn for polishing the manuscript. I appreciate the illustrative work of Sarah Haynes that helps complement many of the stories contained herein.

I'm thankful for the available resources, in print and online, of the Church of Jesus Christ of Latter-day Saints, Brigham Young University, state government and park service agencies and many other organizations.

Lastly, I appreciate the journalists, historians and authors from whose sources I gleaned. As a fellow journalist and author, I know how thankless our job can be at times, especially in the digital world of bloggers and alternative news sources. But I very much appreciate your efforts and writings—most notably, for this book, the fine reporters and editors at both the *Deseret News* and the *Salt Lake Tribune*.

The book and its interpretation on Utah history and events, however, are strictly my own, as are any mistakes or wrong conclusions. That said, I've tried to present the stories as factually as my time and research and understanding would allow. While the task of completing the manuscript at times seemed laborious because of many other pressing demands, I've enjoyed revisiting and learning Utah history and its interesting and sometimes quirky and tragic tales. Now that the book is finished, I hope you enjoy the reading experience. Thanks for giving it a try.

Introduction

History doesn't repeat itself, but it does rhyme.
—Mark Twain

Utah. It wasn't a name the early pioneers had chosen. They wanted to name the territory Deseret—which they did—but when statehood was petitioned, legislators named the new union member Utah, a word that in one Ute vernacular means "top of the mountains."

It's a fitting name, Utah. It's a state full of mountains. One of its most popular ranges, the Wasatch Mountains, stretches across the Great Salt Lake Valley, giving it its eastern wall. On the west side of the valley lie the Oquirrh Mountains, the two ranges forming a true basin or bowl. The pioneers believed that the valley was designed by heaven for a specific purpose: secluding the early Latter-day Saints within this protective basin.

Long before the Mormons arrived, however, many others had experienced this desert bastion, whether they lived here as Indians or traversed here as explorers, fur trappers and missionaries. Thus, when the pioneers arrived in the summer of 1847, the territory that would one day be called Utah already had a history.

This book is not about that history. Nor is it a chronological history of the state or even a snapshot history of Utah. I want to tell you that right off, before you start reading the book or, perchance, before you purchase it at the bookstore. I want you to know what you're getting into before you buy it.

Introduction

As you can see by its size, a true history of Utah would nearly be impossible to tell in such a small volume as this. Like my book *Forgotten Tales of Idaho*, this volume instead is about some of the lesser-known or overlooked tales from the state's history, as recalled in newspaper articles and other sources. This book really is a snapshot of a snapshot of certain stories that, put into the larger puzzle that is Utah, gives us a glimpse of its fascinating history. That puzzle, far from complete, is still being put together.

Forgotten Tales is a presumed title. Chances are you're familiar with some of these stories already. If you're a member of the LDS Church, for instance, you might very well be familiar with some of the stories in Parts I and II, but they are tales that likely would be unfamiliar to a larger Utah audience, thus their inclusion in the book. This book is also not an in-depth study of the stories shared, but rather, the tales are written in a format aimed to offer quick and easy reading for users of this volume. If you're looking for more detailed information, you'll have to look elsewhere. That kind of book is not this one.

It is a book, however, that was fun for me to research and write. I hope, in turn, that you'll find some enjoyment in reading the stories I've selected to share with you in the following pages and that they'll encourage you to uncover some of the many other tales of Utah's colorful and eventful past.

Part I

Mormon Utah

Members of the Church of Jesus Christ of Latter-day Saints first came to the Salt Lake Valley in 1847, when the territory was still part of Mexico. They wanted to name their new home "Deseret," which means honeybee in the Book of Mormon, but when statehood was imminent, legislators petitioned the name Utah. The gentiles may have won that battle, but it was the Mormons who first caught the vision—literally, as we shall see—of living and thriving in the Great Basin and making Utah what it is today. It seems only fitting that we start the book with tales from Latter-day Saint history as they concern the Beehive State. Utah is many things, but in many respects, it's still Mormon Country.

Brigham Young Has the Fever

Just because something is tradition doesn't mean it's historically accurate. Case in point: Pioneer Day. If you don't know the history surrounding this popular day in Utah, you may be led to believe that the Mormon pioneers arrived in the Salt Lake Valley on July 24, 1847. That usually is what you hear, and it is indeed the day Brigham Young and his company of Latter-day Saints, about 148 in all, entered the Great Salt Lake Valley. But they were not the first Mormons to arrive in what later would be known as the Beehive State. That happened three days earlier.

To the Rocky Mountains or Bust

Even before the Church of Jesus Christ of Latter-day Saints was officially organized on April 6, 1830, in Upstate New York, its founder and followers had been persecuted by apostates, naysayers and violent mobs. It was an act of violence that led to the Prophet Joseph Smith's death on June 27, 1844. Those who struck down Smith and his brother, Hyrum, in cold blood while imprisoned in Carthage, Illinois, wrongly believed that the death of Joseph Smith would put an end to Mormonism, a religion not unlike the one Christ established in the New Testament but that was to the anti-Mormons—as Christ's teachings was to the Pharisees in his day—a blasphemous perversion of scriptural intent. When the persecutors saw that the Mormon cause was greater than its Prophet—that the Latter-day Saints continued to amass converts and complete a temple in Nauvoo, Illinois, for instance—they doubled their efforts to persecute and diminish the newfound religion, and the Saints eventually put their boots and wagon wheels to America's overland trails and headed west.

Brigham Young, by appointment and revelation as president of the Quorum of the Twelve Apostles, took charge of the growing church and instructed as many of the Saints as possible to move to the Rocky Mountains. The directive was not entirely his own. Some years before his passing, Joseph Smith allegedly saw in a vision the removal of the Latter-day Saints to the mountainous West. According to one account by Anson Call, an elder in the early church, Smith told the brethren he was with on July 14, 1842, in Montrose, Iowa, that "many things should transpire in the mountains." After taking a drink of cold water, the Prophet allegedly said, "Brethren, this water tastes much like the crystal streams that are running in the Rocky Mountains which some of you" will see.

> *There are some of those standing here that will perform a great work in that land.* [N]*ations of the earth shall be astonished, and many* [people] *of them will be gathered in that land, assisting in building cities and temples, and Israel shall be made to rejoice. But, before you see this day, you will pass through scenes that are but little understood by you. This people will be made to mourn, multitudes will die and many will apostatize, but the priesthood shall prevail over all its enemies, triumph over the devil and be established upon the earth, nevermore to be thrown down.*

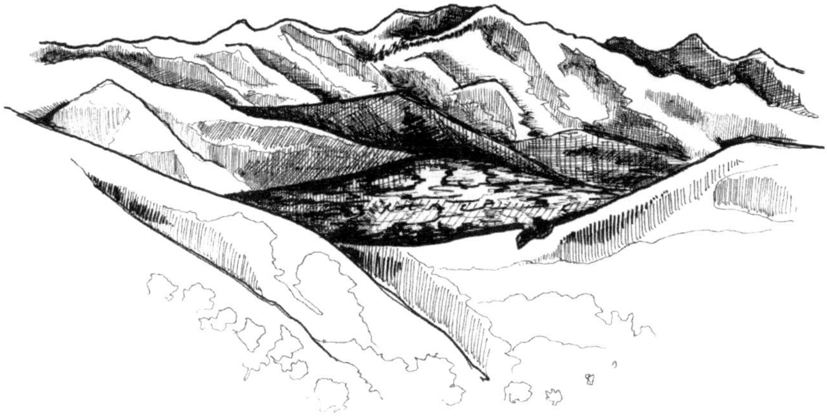

The mission of a prophet is, among other things, to prophesy. As we recall Mormon history in light of the aforementioned prophecy, it is easy to see its fulfillment, even down to the Mormon converts and others who "gathered in that land" and helped build "cities and temples." It is one of many prophecies made by Joseph Smith that have been fulfilled. Joseph may have seen in vision the Rocky Mountains, but he would never see them in person. The responsibility to lead the Saints on their westward journey fell to Brigham Young, Smith's successor and the man who has been named a "Modern Moses" for accomplishing the great modern-day exodus and who also rightly has been called a colonizer.

Young, whom history often paints as a fiery, pulpit-pounding polygamist, was in reality a stern but humble man who was apt to give credit where credit was due. In this case, Young said that he never intended to move beyond what was known at the time as America's western frontier. "Joseph contemplated the move for years before it took place," he said, further clarifying that the modern exodus was a moment of divine origin. "I do not wish men to understand I had anything to do with our being moved here, that was the providence of the Almighty; it was the power of God that wrought out salvation for this people, I never could have devised such a plan."

The Exodus Begins

The Latter-day Saints began making plans to move west as early as 1844, but it wasn't until February 1846 that the first company of pioneers left Nauvoo, a city inspired by Joseph Smith wherein the Saints built their second temple. They would not hit the trail, in fact, until the temple was finished, so they could partake of the sacred ceremonies within it. Only after they received their endowments did they pack up as much of their belongings as they could carry and, once again, leave their homes. Some pioneer companies were scheduled to leave in the late winter or early spring of 1846, but eager to leave the mobs behind, they advanced their plans before some companies were fully prepared. Young, who left on February 4, 1846, with some three thousand Latter-day Saints, expected to reach Salt Lake by the following winter but had to scrap his original goal and split the journey into two sections: Nauvoo, Illinois, to Omaha, Nebraska, in 1846 and Omaha to the Salt Lake Valley in 1847.

The trail that would take them west, which had been scouted earlier by a vanguard company ordered by Young, stretched some 1,200 miles through deserts and prairies, across rivers and over mountain passes. They may have left their persecutors behind, but now new trials faced the Latter-day Saints. Volumes have been filled with the hardships the pioneers endured as they sought their Zion. Many of them, young and old alike, perished on the trail long before their eyes could behold their new intended home in the Rockies. Even for those who survived, the journey was an arduous one.

"The first part of the journey to the Salt Lake Valley was very difficult for the first group of pioneers," reads information in a church study manual. "It took them 131 days to travel 300 miles across Iowa. A year later another group of pioneers took only 111 days to travel 1050 miles from Iowa all the way to the Great Salt Lake Valley."

Apostles Erastus Snow and Orson Pratt, members of the vanguard scouting company, entered the Salt Lake Valley on July 21—three days before Young and his company arrived. It is reported that after establishing camp and exploring the valley, Elder Pratt said a prayer in which he dedicated the land to the Lord. Thus, even before Brigham Young saw the valley and approved it as the new home for the dispersed Latter-day Saints, the first company of pioneers had already sanctioned it their Zion.

Behold, the Valley

It was a Saturday when Brigham Young saw the Great Salt Lake Valley for the first time from the mouth of present-day Emigration Canyon, properly named for the historic event that took place there that day. Perhaps the sight before him looked familiar—the expansive terrain, the valley's central river and its glistening salt sea—for at one time he, too, supposedly saw the Great Salt Lake Valley in a vision, giving ample clarification for his famous statement: "This is the right place." Elder Wilford Woodruff was with him when he uttered the phrase, as were other brethren of the church, and recorded the experience. Young, not feeling well, was both anxious and eager to make the journey's end. He turned his attention to the wagon master: "Drive on!"

Young gave the order from the back of the wagon in which he lay with a bout of Rocky Mountain spotted fever, which, according to the modern Centers for Disease Control and Prevention, can be a severe or even fatal illness caused by the bite of an infected tick species. Typical symptoms include abdominal pain, headache, fever, muscle pain and vomiting.

What a relief it must have been for the Saints, and perhaps especially for President Young, to finally arrive at their promised land. "God has shown me that this is the spot to locate this people, and here is where they will prosper," he later told those who were with him that day. "As the Saints gather here and get strong enough to possess the land, God will temper the climate and we shall build a city and a temple to the Most High God in this place. We will extend our settlements to the east and west, to the north and to the south, and we will build towns and cities by the hundreds, and thousands of Saints will gather in from the nations of the earth. This will become the great highway of nations."

Like Joseph Smith had done before him, Brigham Young had uttered a prophecy about the Latter-day Saints in the Rocky Mountains. The Mormons extended their settlements and built towns and cities, and hundreds of thousands of them gathered in Utah to make it their home. The early Saints also were privy to build not one temple—which was constructed in the heart of downtown Salt Lake City—but several across the state. Young first proclaimed the building of the Salt Lake Temple just four days after he arrived, on July 28, at which time he also gave instruction for the grid pattern of the city. "Here is the 40 acres for the temple," he said, striking his cane into the ground. "The city can be laid out perfectly square, north, south, east, and west." Wilford Woodruff, who was with him that day, as he was on many occasions, placed a marker at the very spot where Young had placed his cane.

When it came time to start construction on the temple five years later, it would be a mountainous task to which the Saints applied themselves. Before that time arrived, however, the brethren had another mountain to climb, this time a literal one called Ensign Peak. At its tops, an ensign would be waved in the form of a rented coat, if only briefly, signifying the virtues of Mormonism and the promise of a new era in the kingdom's history.

AN ENSIGN TO THE WORLD

While at base camp at what is now the modern site of the Salt Lake City and County Building at Washington Square, in the midst of the massive Wasatch Mountains, Brigham Young observed a mountain peak to the north. Something about it caught his attention. It looked familiar. Pointing his finger toward the peak, he told the brethren who were with him, Wilford Woodruff among them, "I want to go there."

Young was still recovering from a bout of Rocky Mountain spotted fever, so his request may have surprised the brethren. When Brother Brigham spoke, however, you listened. Several of the brethren prepared their horses and rode to the mountain. And then they started to climb.

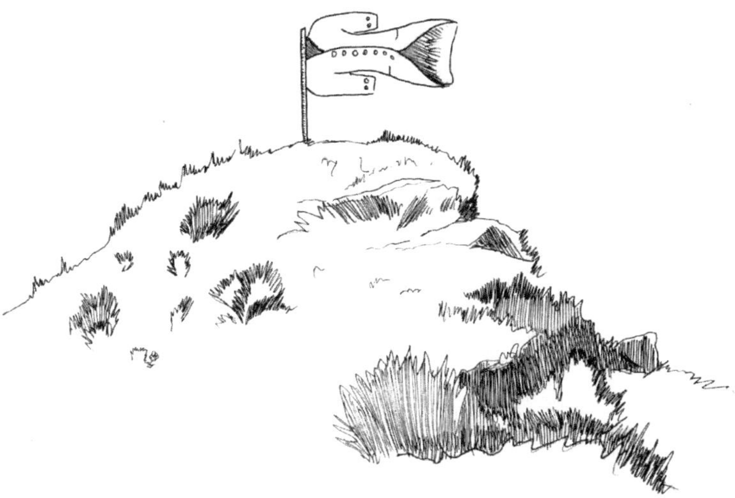

Woodruff was the first to reach the top; it took Young longer because of his condition. Once there, he once more gazed across the valley, just as he had done from another peak while in the back of a wagon days earlier. Then, without fanfare or preamble, he named the hill. "This is Ensign Peak," Young said, explaining that there was a reason it looked familiar to him.

"There is historical evidence to support that before the Saints entered the valley, Joseph Smith, in vision, showed Brigham Young the Salt Lake Valley and the layout of the city from the vantage point of Ensign Peak," Elder Loren C. Dunn wrote in a February 6, 1993 *Church News* article. So, in the interim between July 24, when Young entered the valley, and July 28, when he spoke of building the Salt Lake Temple, "he climbed to the top of Ensign Peak, possibly to confirm what he had previously seen."

"A Banner Is Unfurled"

The name Ensign Peak is symbolic. One of the meanings of the word *ensign*, according to Merriam-Webster, is "a flag that is flown…as the symbol of nationality and that may also be flown with a distinctive badge added to its design." The word is used in scripture as a spiritual emblem, such as representing the gospel or church, and to which people of faith flock. That was the meaning of the Old Testament prophet Isaiah, in whom Latter-day Saints have a particular interest, when he wrote in Isaiah 5:26–27 and the Second Book of Nephi 15:26–27 that in the latter days the Lord would "lift up an ensign to the nations from far, and will signal to them from the ends of the earth: and behold, they shall come with speed swiftly; none shall be weary or stumble among them."

The gospel—not Utah—is the ensign, according to Mormon belief. Yet the church had to have headquarters, and the Salt Lake Valley was chosen as the site, thus also becoming an ensign of sorts. From here, again according to a Mormon perspective, the banner of peace and truth would be unfurled and shine like a beacon to all the world. From here, the gospel message would roll forth to the nations of the earth.

"It Waves to All the World"

What the brethren did atop Ensign Peak that Monday in early church history is reminiscent of another prophet's banner that was raised to strengthen the faith of a weary army of God-fearing men. The Book of Mormon's Captain Moroni, chief commander of the Nephite army at a time of dissention and conflict, called his makeshift flag his "Title of Liberty." After hard-fought battles, his army was growing weary. Captain Moroni became angry with Amalickiah, the leader of the opposition, and with the evil tides of warfare that seemed relentless. The very freedoms of the Nephites were at stake. Knowing when enough was enough, the Nephite commander, in a moment of passion, "rent his coat; and he took a piece thereof, and wrote upon it—In memory of our God, our religion, and freedom, and our peace, our wives, and our children—and he fastened it upon the end of a pole," as related in Alma 46:12. The emblem, and the act of raising it, gave courage to his men. They went forth and fought the good fight of faith in the midst of heavy warfare.

George Washington did something similar during the Revolutionary War. That's not so unusual considering that in the historic perspective of war, most every band of soldiers has a flag or banner that represents its political or religious position. In retelling America's fight for independence in his memorable book *1776*, historian David McCullough wrote:

> *At the Cambridge headquarters, Washington declared in his general orders for New Year's Day the commencement of a "new army which in every point of view is entirely continental." And thus the army, though still 90 percent a New England army, had a name, the Continental Army.*
>
> *He stressed the hope that "the importance of the great Cause we are engaged in will be deeply impressed upon every man's mind." Everything "dear and valuable to freeman" was at stake, he said, calling on their patriotism to rally morale and commitment, but also expressing exactly what he felt.*
>
> *With the crash of a 13-gun salute, he raised a new flag in honor of the birthday of the new army—a flag of thirteen red and white stripes, with the British colors (the crosses of St. George and St. Andrew) represented in the upper corner. When the British in Boston saw it flying from Prospect Hill, they at first mistook it for a flag of surrender.*

As history knows, it was anything but a flag of surrender. Even though it took America eight years to gain its independence—from 1775, when the war started, to 1783, when it ended—the states had won their first major battle as a unified country in 1776.

Fast-forward to 1847, Utah. After Young proclaimed the hill's name Ensign Peak, he said, "Now, Brethren, organize your exploring parties, so as to be safe from Indians; go and explore where you will, and you will come back every time and say this is the best place." Moments later, it is reported that Heber C. Kimball exclaimed, "We will sometime raise an ensign here!" Then, taking a yellow bandana, he fastened it to a walking cane belonging to Willard Richards and held it above their heads as they prayed.

So memorable was the moment that Joel Hills Johnson, one of the early pioneers with a poet's knack, was inspired to pen a hymn about the occasion called "Deseret," later changed to "High on the Mountain Top." The popular hymn signifies the symbolism of Ensign Peak, the yellow bandana that served a greater purpose that day in church history and the true ensign that is the gospel:

High on the mountain top a banner is unfurled.
Ye nations, now look up, it waves to all the world.
In Deseret's sweet, peaceful land,
On Zion's mount, behold it stand!

For God remembers still his promise made of old
That he on Zion's hill Truth's standard would unfold!
Her light should there attract the gaze
Of all the world in latter days.

PROTECTING THE GREAT TEMPLE

Fulfillment of Brigham Young's prophecy of July 28, 1847, in which he proclaimed that a temple would one day stand in the center of town, began on April 6, 1853, when the cornerstone was laid for what would become the Salt Lake Temple. It would take forty years for the granite temple to be completed, a celebration in which Young would never partake. The great Mormon colonizer passed away on August 29, 1877. But he oversaw twenty-four years of the temple's construction, including perhaps the project's most challenging time. It was a trial that quite literally rocked its very foundation, but in hindsight, it helped fortify the temple for years to come.

Although it was the first temple announced in the territory, it was the fourth one to be completed—St. George, Manti and Logan Temples were finished before the Salt Lake Temple was dedicated on April 6, 1893. Unlike modern construction projects, which use the equipment and skills of professional contractors, it was members of the church who shaped the granite facility into a truly magnificent religious icon in the heart of the Desert West. With the keen foresight of an entrepreneur—or of a prophet, as the Latter-day Saints are wont to call him—Young enlisted the help of missionaries to not only spread the gospel message abroad but also seek converts of many skills and professions who could help the Saints build their Zion, including their great temple. Skilled artisans, masons, sculptors and other Mormon converts from Europe and other places came to the Salt Lake Valley, where they joined the cause.

Burying the Foundation

That most challenging of episodes in the building of the Salt Lake Temple, and one of the more remarkable feats of its construction, occurred during Young's administration. The story is portrayed in the LDS film *Mountain of the Lord*, in which a segment of the movie depicts a perceived threat and the great lengths to which the Mormons went in order to protect their temple.

Upon hearing that President James Buchanan had sent a band of U.S. Army soldiers to Salt Lake to put down a supposed insurrection by the Mormons, Young did something that may have taken many church members by surprise: he directed that the temple's foundation be buried.

The reason the Latter-day Saints came to the Rocky Mountains was to escape persecution and build a community in which they could worship God according to the dictates of their own conscience, unmolested by persecution, mob violence and government interference. It was an ideal ambition, but one that in the real world of the 1800s was, in some ways, not realistic. The threat of persecution—and, in some instances, persecution itself—followed them. Knowing all too well how the church had been treated by the government in Missouri, Illinois and other parts Midwest, Young had no intention of allowing the same mistreatment of the Saints in their new home. Burying the foundation seemed like the logical thing to do to keep their work from prying eyes.

Members of the church did as Young commanded. In 1858, the foundation was covered with dirt, and the soil was prepared to look like a farmer's field. Only when the soldiers left, and tensions relaxed, did Young direct that the foundation be uncovered. When that job was completed—

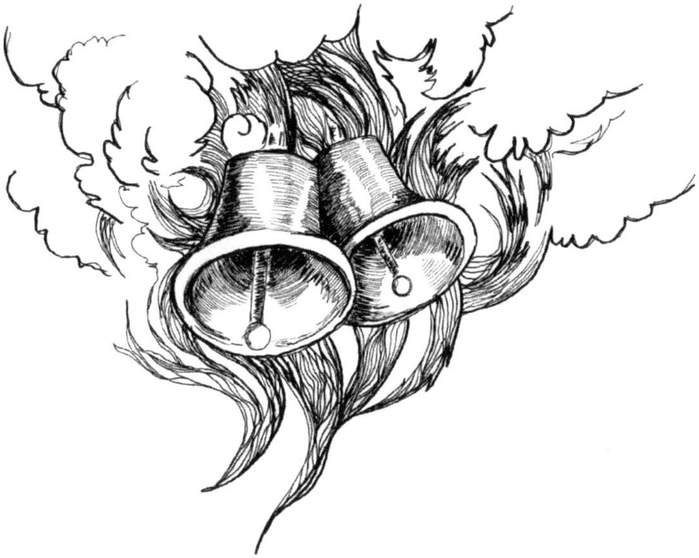

no easy task with simple shovels and hand tools—it was revealed that cracks had formed in the foundation, causing work on the temple to halt. The architect, Truman O. Angell, told President Young that the foundation was not strong enough to support the weight of a granite temple.

President Young once said that there never was a temple built without the bells of hell ringing. "We completed a temple in Kirtland and in Nauvoo; and did not the Monster of hell toll all the time we were building them?" he said on March 3, 1861, in the Salt Lake Tabernacle. "They did, every week and every day." Now they seemed to be chiming again. And yet he knew that his commission as a prophet was to help bring the Latter-day Saints the saving ordinances of the gospel. This new challenge was disappointing but not unexpected.

As touchingly portrayed in *Mountain of the Lord*, Young said to Angell, "I shall not move from this spot until I know what it is I am to do." Later that evening, Young was approached by Brother Woodruff, who informed him that it was believed by the construction workers that cracks were caused by using too much mortar, and settling caused the cracks to spread. Woodruff said he feared that the entire foundation would have to be removed and the project started again.

"What more can there be?" Young replied. "Nine years we have struggled to build this temple. We have suffered humiliating poverty and persecution. Our brethren have blistered in the summer sun, scalded in their own sweat. They've shuttered and soaked through torrential thunderstorms with lightning dancing all about them. They've frozen off fingers and toes in winter's blasts. We have stood against the gaping jaws of hell itself. Yet there are nights that I lie awake for fear that I will never live to see this temple dedicated. I expect this temple to stand through the millennium, Wilford, so the saints of future generations may go in and receive their endowments."

Then, as revelation dawned, Young's demeanor changed. Instead of the downcast look to his face just moments before, he now set his chin to the task at hand. "You were right, my friend," he said. "We will take up the foundation and begin again." From that day forward, it was Angell's responsibility to measure and specify each stone for its position in the temple, a process that continued throughout the entire construction. The early church members showed what can happen when determination and patience prevail: they worked on the Salt Lake Temple for more than the next two decades, completing it in the spring of 1893—fifty years from when the project began.

A Spiritual Temple

As Brother Brigham feared, he wasn't present to see the temple's completion. But Wilford Woodruff, who was with President Young on that day forty-six years earlier when he announced the future temple, saw its fulfillment and offered its dedicatory prayer. The Salt Lake Temple was completed in April 1893, with a public open house held on April 5. Dedication ceremonies followed between April 6 and 24. Woodruff, who by now had become the fourth president of the church, in part prayed:

> *O Lord, we regard with intense and indescribable feelings the completion of this sacred house. Deign to accept this the fourth temple which Thy covenant children have been assisted by Thee in erecting in these mountains. In past ages Thou didst inspire with Thy Holy Spirit Thy servants, the prophets, to speak of the time in the latter days when the mountain of the Lord's house should be established in the tops of the mountains, and should be exalted above the hills. We thank Thee that we have had the glorious opportunity of contributing to the fulfillment of these visions of Thine ancient seers, and that Thou hast condescended*

> *to permit us to take part in the great work. And as this portion of Thy servants' words has thus so marvelously been brought to pass, we pray Thee, with increased faith and renewed hope, that all their words with regard to Thy great work in gathering Thine Israel and building up Thy kingdom on earth in the last days may be as amply fulfilled, and that, O Lord, speedily.*
>
> *...Heavenly Father, when Thy people shall not have the opportunity of entering this holy house to offer their supplications unto Thee, and they are oppressed and in trouble, surrounded by difficulties or assailed by temptation and shall turn their faces towards this Thy holy house and ask Thee for deliverance, for help, for Thy power to be extended in their behalf, we beseech Thee, to look down from Thy holy habitation in mercy and tender compassion upon them, and listen to their cries. Or when the children of Thy people, in years to come, shall be separated, through any cause, from this place, and their hearts shall turn in remembrance of Thy promises to this holy Temple, and they shall cry unto Thee from the depths of their affliction and sorrow to extend relief and deliverance to them, we humbly entreat Thee to Turn Thine ear in mercy to them; hearken to their cries, and grant unto them the blessings for which they ask.*

The pinnacle of Latter-day Saint worship takes place in the temple. It is where, according to Mormon theology, husbands and wives marry not only for time but eternity and, in that union, have their children bound to them forever as an eternal family. Temples are where doctrines of the gospel are better explained, where instruction relating to mankind's purpose on earth is given and where the teachings and mission of Jesus Christ are better clarified and deepened. Temples are facilities specially dedicated to the Lord and his latter-day work. And according to Mormon teachings, temples are places where He and His angels may visit, which they often have done, according to historical accounts of the church.

Several recorded instances of spiritual manifestations have taken place in the Salt Lake Temple. President Wilford Woodruff, the one who dedicated the temple after it was finished, recorded a dream he had of the temple before it was completed:

> *I dreamed last night that the LD Saints were holding a great Conference at Salt Lake City at the great Temple and thousands of Mechanics were laboring hard to finish the Temple. I was requested to open the Conference As I was an Exile and they might not have me with them long. The Key*

> *of the Temple was given me to open it. As I went to the door A large Company were assembled and I overtook Presid[en]t Brigham Young and He asked what the matter was with the great Company at the Door. Some one Answered the Elders did not want to Let the people into the Temple. He said Oh, oh, oh and turned to me & said let all[,] all into the Temple who seek for Salvation. I saw several who were Dead and among the Number my wife Phebe. I Believe there is some meaning to this dream.*

During the dedication ceremonies, many church members reported having spiritual experiences. Susa Young Gates said that she saw "radiant light" shine on the countenance of Joseph F. Smith as he spoke to the audience, and because the weather was not such to emit such light on his frame, she "was sure that I had seen the actual Presence of the Holy Spirit, focused upon the features of the beloved leader." Bardella S. Curtis, a choir member, claimed that she saw "the veil between mortality and high heaven drawn aside."

The most memorable recorded experience took place inside the temple about five years after its dedication. This bit of history comes from the life of Lorenzo Snow, who at the deathbed of Wilford Woodruff was anxious about bearing the Prophet's mantle. Snow, who at the time was president of the Quorum of the Twelve Apostles, "knelt at the sacred altar in the Holy of Holies in the Salt Lake Temple and there plead to the Lord to spare President Woodruff's life," his daughter, Alice, penned in her journal. "President Snow prayed that President Woodruff might outlive him and that the great responsibility of Church leadership would not fall upon his shoulders. But he also promised the Lord that he would devotedly perform any duty required at his hands."

On the evening of September 2, 1898, after finding out that President Woodruff had passed, President Snow once more retired to a room in the Salt Lake Temple and poured out his heart in solemn prayer. "Thy will be done," he prayed. "I have not sought this responsibility but if it be Thy will, I now present myself before Thee for Thy guidance and instruction. I ask that Thou show me what Thou wouldst have me do."

After he ended his prayer, he expected an answer—"some special manifestation from the Lord"—but none came, and his heart sank. He arose from the altar, disappointed that he had not received an answer, something to reassure him. He left the room and passed through the Celestial Room and into the large corridor just outside. To his surprise, it was here that he received an answer.

It is from President Snow's granddaughter, Allie Young Pond, that we receive the account of the heavenly manifestation and the circumstances that led to her grandfather sharing the experience with her:

> *One evening while I was visiting Grandpa Snow in his room in the Salt Lake Temple, I remained until the door keepers had gone and the night-watchmen had not yet come in, so grandpa said he would take me to the main front entrance and let me out that way. He got his bunch of keys from his dresser. After we left his room and while we were still in the large corridor leading into the celestial room, I was walking several steps ahead of grandpa when he stopped me and said:*
>
> *"Wait a moment, Allie. I want to tell you something. It was right here that the Lord Jesus Christ appeared to me at the time of the death of President Woodruff. He instructed me to go right ahead and reorganize the First Presidency of the Church at once and not wait as had been done after the death of the previous presidents, and that I was to succeed President Woodruff.*
>
> *"He stood right here, about three feet above the floor. It looked as though he stood on a plate of solid gold."*
>
> *Grandpa told me what a glorious personage the Savior is and described His hands, feet, countenance and beautiful White Robes, all of which were of such a glory of whiteness and brightness that he could hardly gaze upon Him.*
>
> *"Now granddaughter, I want you to remember that this is the testimony of your grandfather, that he told you with his own lips that he actually saw the Savior, here in the temple, and talked with him face to face."*

Engraved onto the temple are many symbolisms, as well as the bold engraving, HOLINESS TO THE LORD/THE HOUSE OF THE LORD. Latter-day Saints verily believe that their specially dedicated temples are sacred sanctuaries where Jesus Christ makes himself known to his prophet and the pure in heart. The spiritual stories shared in this chapter, just a few in the annals of the temple's history, seem to affirm this to the believing Latter-day Saints. And in great measure they have Brigham Young to thank for them. If not for a prophet's vision, his foresight and gumption to have the foundation buried in order to protect it, the cracks may not have been revealed until much later in the construction process, causing the work to be delayed further or halted altogether.

The Deseret Alphabet

No one ever said the Latter-day Saints were lazy. It's a moniker that, as a whole, just doesn't fit the members of this ambitious and enterprising faith. There are many instances in LDS Church history that affirm this, including the story about the Deseret Alphabet.

The word *Deseret*, an unusual name to those not of the faith, springs up in several instances in church history. When the pioneers arrived in the Salt Lake Valley, for instance, they wanted to name their new home Deseret, a name taken from the Book of Mormon that means honeybee. Since honeybees are industrious, it was the perfect motto for the ambitious Mormons, who believed that to be idle is ungodly. It's through work, coupled with faith, that great things come to pass.

One of the more ambitious projects proposed by Brigham Young began in 1852, just five years after the pioneers arrived, when he commissioned members of the board of regents of the University of Deseret to create a new alphabet.

Tough English

English isn't the easiest language to learn. It has, in fact, been called one of the harder languages for non-English speakers to learn because, simply put, there are many conundrums in the English language. An article by the Oxford Royale Academy, a British university in Oxford, England, shares some examples:

> *There is no ham in hamburger, for instance, or apple or pine in pineapple. If teachers taught, why don't preachers praught? If a vegetarian eats vegetables, what does a humanitarian eat? And while "overlook" and "oversee" have opposite meanings, "look" and "see" mean the same thing. As native speakers, we rarely stop to think how illogical many of the things we say really are—we're just used to them. Unless you've been brought up speaking English, how can you possibly begin to learn all these oddities? It's little wonder that people trying to learn English end up feeling confused. But it gets worse.* [The article goes on to explain many other difficulties that learners of the language confront, such as the rules "i before e except after c" and the pronunciation of words like *rough*, *tough* and *knife*, all of which have silent letters.]

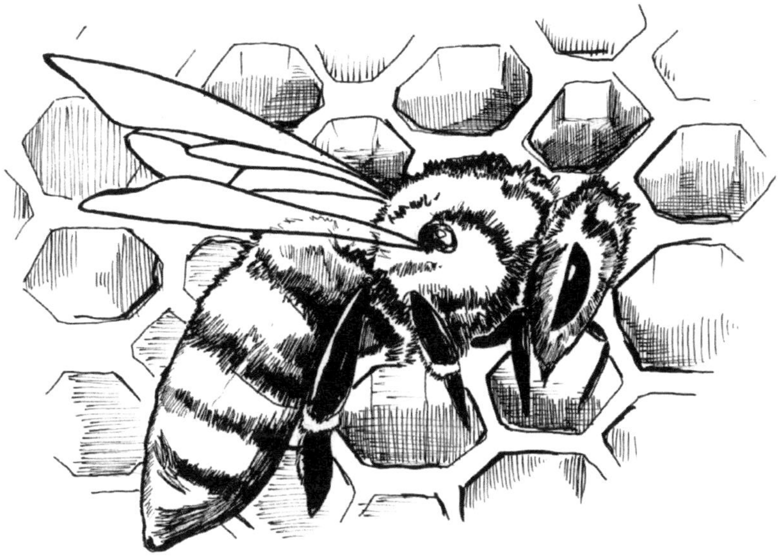

In another sense, however, English is a welcoming language, having adopted many ancient Greek and Latin words. But that is not all. *Effective Language Learning* describes English as being an "Indo-European language of the Germanic language family," noting that the language was developed by "many influences over the last few thousand years." As such, "there are hundreds of languages that have contributed to the formation of the English language."

In a nutshell, English is a vast and comprehensive language. For many people, past and present, it is a tough language to learn. In his day, Brigham Young wanted to change that.

Ambitious Project

Leave it to Brother Brigham—one of the most ambitious and industrious historical figures of record—to aspire to create a whole new alphabet. His purpose in doing so wasn't to just fiddle with the art of language and letters. "The idea was to develop a sort of universal system especially so that foreign-language-speaking converts could learn to read English more easily," reads an entry by Samuel C. Monson in the *Encyclopedia of Mormonism*.

> *The final version of the Deseret Alphabet utilized thirty-eight characters corresponding to sounds of English. Like Noah Webster and other early Americans who studied language, Brigham Young objected to sounding the letter* a *differently in the spellings of the mate, father, fall, man, and many. In this, he was apparently influenced by studying shorthand with his secretary George D. Watt, who had studied systems of shorthand and spelling reform based on phonemes, the significant sounds of English, under Isaac Pitman.*
>
> *The Regents discussed letter forms and sounds to be represented. The forms finally adopted were unfamiliar and unadaptable to cursive writing. The range of basic English sounds was close to present-day analyses, but the schwa (the unaccented, reduced vowel in idea, traded, ratify, biology, upon) was omitted, leading to respellings based upon traditional spelling.*

Think of the task at hand. Those he had commissioned to create the alphabet were not traditional linguists, and yet they accomplished a remarkable feat.

Once the alphabet was created in 1854, Young had it taught in schools. "It will be the means of introducing uniformity in our orthography," he said, "and the years ahead that are now required to learn to read and spell can be devoted to other studies." Several books were published using the alphabet—which very much resembles a foreign alphabet if you're not familiar with it—including the Book of Mormon. The alphabet today can be found in historical records such as some church meeting minutes and journals and on some coins that were minted at the time. There's even at least one headstone at the Cedar City Cemetery, belonging to John Thomas Morris, engraved with the alphabet's characters. But because of excessive costs to print the characters, it wasn't feasible to continue using the alphabet, and it was eventually discontinued.

Revisiting the Alphabet

Although it never succeeded the way Brigham Young had anticipated, the alphabet has stood the test of time in that more modern scholars have recognized the consistency and ease of learning the characters. Something that might please Brother Brigham: linguist students at the University of

California–Berkley learned the alphabet in just two months, and a proposal was submitted to the Library of Congress in 2015 for a new Deseret Romanization table, which was released in February 2016.

Prisoner for Polygamy

When the Prophet Joseph Smith proposed the practice of plural marriage, saying that it was an ancient biblical practice that the Lord commanded be started again as part of the "restoration of all things," it wasn't a law he was excited about. He was married to a supportive wife whom he loved and also supported. He claimed the teaching came as a revelation from God, not of his own mind, and one that carried a heavy burden for the Prophet and those he later asked to participate in it. It caused consternation and division among members, and ultimately it was one of the teachings that led a mob to assassinate the Prophet in 1844. But those who embraced the practice believed it was a commandment revealed anew.

"This principle was among the most challenging aspects of the Restoration—for Joseph personally and the other Church members," reads an essay on the LDS website. "Plural marriage tested faith and provoked controversy and opposition. Few Latter-day Saints initially welcomed the restoration of a biblical practice entirely foreign to their sensibilities. But many later testified of powerful spiritual experiences that helped them overcome their hesitation and gave them courage to accept this practice." Likewise, when the LDS Church abandoned the practice of plural marriage, some members had a difficult time giving it up.

The church officially abandoned polygamy in 1890 after President Wilford Woodruff issued what is called the Manifesto, but it started prohibiting plural marriages as early as 1889 in Utah. By the following May, the U.S. Supreme Court upheld the constitutionality of the Edmunds-Tuck Act, passed in 1887, which restricted some access of the LDS Church. In brief, Woodruff created the Manifesto—a document abolishing the practice of polygamous marriages in the church—because of government oppression. Taking the situation under consideration, President Woodruff saw that if the church did not abandon the practice, the oppression would continue, and eventually the church would lose its assets, including its temples, and dissolve instead of grow. The church, which also believes in obeying the laws of the land, had to fall in line with the federal mandate.

"I hereby declare my intention to submit to those laws," President Woodruff explained in the Manifesto, listed as Declaration 1 in the church's Doctrines and Covenants, "and to use my influence with the members of the Church over which I preside to have them do likewise." Thus, "I now publicly declare that my advice to the Latter-day Saints is to refrain from contracting any marriage forbidden by the law of the land."

Some members didn't accept the mandate, believing that the law of God should supersede the law of man; some believed President Woodruff had become a fallen prophet, having been pressured by the government to forsake a God-given principle. Woodruff, on more than one occasion, said that he did not personally authorize any polygamous marriages after he issued the Manifesto, but several members performed plural marriage ceremonies in secret even after the Manifesto was made public. At least one ceremony was performed in the Endowment House in Salt Lake City, "but I have not been able to learn who performed the ceremony," the Prophet wrote in the Manifesto; whatever "was done in this matter was without my knowledge." Woodruff, after learning of the incident, instructed that the Endowment House be "taken down without delay," so adamant was he about keeping the new law. "Like the beginning of plural marriage in the Church, the end of the practice was a process rather than a single event," noted the church essay about the early practice of plural marriage. "Revelation came 'line upon line, precept upon precept.'"

During the time it was church-authorized, however, Woodruff was a staunch supporter of the cause. So was a man named George Reynolds, as were other early brethren of the church, who went to great lengths to protect it.

A Spiritual Journey

The Latter-day Saints had fled the Midwest because of persecution, but now they were facing similar trials in Utah thanks to polygamy and the 1862 Morrill Anti-Bigamy Act, which prohibited the practice of plural marriage. The Mormons believed it was an unconstitutional law, one that should—and eventually would—be overturned. So, along with the U.S. attorney from Utah, they agreed to provide a test case against it. George Reynolds, who had married his second wife, Amelia Schofield, in 1874, was asked to be the church's defendant, and he agreed. It was a decision that would try his patience and faith, but one that ultimately would propel him to an even higher spiritual plateau.

Reynolds was indicted for bigamy by a grand jury on October 23, 1874. The following April 1, he was sentenced to one year in prison. He was indicted a second time on October 30, 1875, and on December 9 was sentenced to two years in prison plus hard labor. The Utah Supreme Court upheld the conviction on June 13, 1876, but the church appealed it to the U.S. Supreme Court. That didn't happen until 1878, however, and the following January, the court made its ruling that it would sustain the Morrill Anti-Bigamy Act. The LDS Church's practice of plural marriage was not, the Supreme Court said, protected under the Constitution.

Reynolds went to prison, but as biographer Bruce A. Van Orden explained in the August 1986 edition of *Ensign* magazine, the hard-labor clause was revoked and his sentence was shortened to eighteen months. He spent most of his sentence at the Utah Territorial Penitentiary.

Van Orden, who wrote a full biography of Reynolds called *A Prisoner for Conscience' Sake*, goes on in his article to explain that "George was regarded as a 'prisoner for conscience' sake,' and prayers in his behalf were offered throughout the Church. Just before Brother Reynolds entered prison, President John Taylor pronounced a blessing on him. The Holy Spirit would rest upon him, promised President Taylor, to enlighten him and other Church members regarding scriptural understanding."

The blessing seemed to have had a profound impact on Reynolds's life and circumstances, for it was in prison that his mind seemed to become enlightened by passages from the scriptures. While wearing black-and-white prison garb, Brother Reynolds made perhaps his most significant contribution to the Church—and it had nothing to do with plural marriage and everything to do with Mormon letters.

He began an earnest study of the Book of Mormon and penned passages and thoughts about the verses he'd read, sometimes "transcribing passages… at the rate of as many as 350 per day," according to Van Orden. By the time he was released from prison on January 20, 1881, he had completed twenty-five thousand entries in what would become *A Complete Concordance to the Book of Mormon*, an exhaustive volume on Mormons' most sacred book. During his lifetime, Reynolds also wrote several other books on topics related to the Book of Mormon and church doctrine.

In 1890, the same year Wilford Woodruff issued the Manifesto, President Woodruff asked Brother Reynolds to serve as a member of the Council of the Seventy. Interestingly, even after spending eighteen months in prison for polygamy, Reynolds married a third wife, Mary Goold, in 1885. He died of meningitis in Salt Lake City on August 9, 1909.

The LDS Church's position on marriage today is monogamy—the union of one man and one woman—and it does not condone the practice of taking multiple wives. But at one time it did, just as God did at times in the biblical past. George Reynolds was a believer, and he stood bold and proud of those beliefs, if not humbled by their controversy. The period in which the church condoned plural marriage was a trying time for members, perhaps especially for Reynolds for being the test case for it, but it also was a scripturally enlightening time for him.

TWAIN ON THE MORMONS

You know him as Mark Twain, but his real name was Samuel Clemens, and from his early writings, it appears he wasn't fond of Mormons. Twain visited Utah in 1861 with his older brother, Orion Clemens, who was on assignment as secretary of the newly created Nevada Territory, but in order to better understand Twain's response to his visit to Utah, you first must know a little about the author himself.

The writer of such classics as *The Adventures of Tom Sawyer* and *Adventures of Huckleberry Finn* also at one time worked as a newspaper reporter. In reality, the word "reporter" should be used rather loosely in describing Twain's journalism. At least once, Twain acknowledged that when he wrote about a topic, he often tried to find its absurdity, choosing to flavor his stories with humor instead of fact. This was so whether he was writing correspondence columns for the *Sacramento Union* or writing about the Latter-day Saints. Although he was a marvelous writer of fiction, he wasn't always the best at getting the whole news story right—he was a satirist more than a reporter. If he were alive today, Twain would be a great blogger. In his book *Roughing It*, he wrote an account of his visit to Salt Lake City and his impressions of the Latter-day Saints and their theology as he viewed them. His accounts are absurd and rather quirky, two adjectives that could also apply to the way he viewed the Mormons. Twain seemed impressed by the rugged beauty of the Salt Lake Valley and the neatness and cleanliness of the Mormon community. Such a well-organized city told him that the Latter-day Saints, if nothing else, were an industrious lot who valued hard work. These impressions, however, did little to discourage him from seeing the faith as a peculiar, if not colorful, religion and writing about it from that perspective.

After his visit to Utah, Twain wrote with such great buffoonery about alcohol, polygamy and Brigham Young that his writings, as one scholar has noted, helped incite anti-Mormon biases against the church for some years afterward. Interestingly, Twain didn't write about his two-day visit to Salt Lake City until about ten years afterward. It is said that when he began to write of his Utah tales, he asked his brother, Orion, in a letter if he remembered much from the trip because, the author admitted, he did not. Twain also at one time in his life admitted that he was not a fan of the Mormon religion, but he seemed to find great amusement satirizing it.

Twain's approach to the LDS faith is interesting, since he seemed to make it a focus of at least some personal study, including reading the Book of Mormon. He once wrote sarcastically of the book's Three Witnesses, whose testimony now appears in the introductory pages of Mormonism's sacred volume, that "when a man tells me that he has seen the engravings which are upon the plates and not only that, but an angel was there at the time and saw them see him and probably took his receipt for it, I am very far on the road to conviction no matter whether I have ever heard of that man before or not, and even if I do not know the name of the angel or his nationality either."

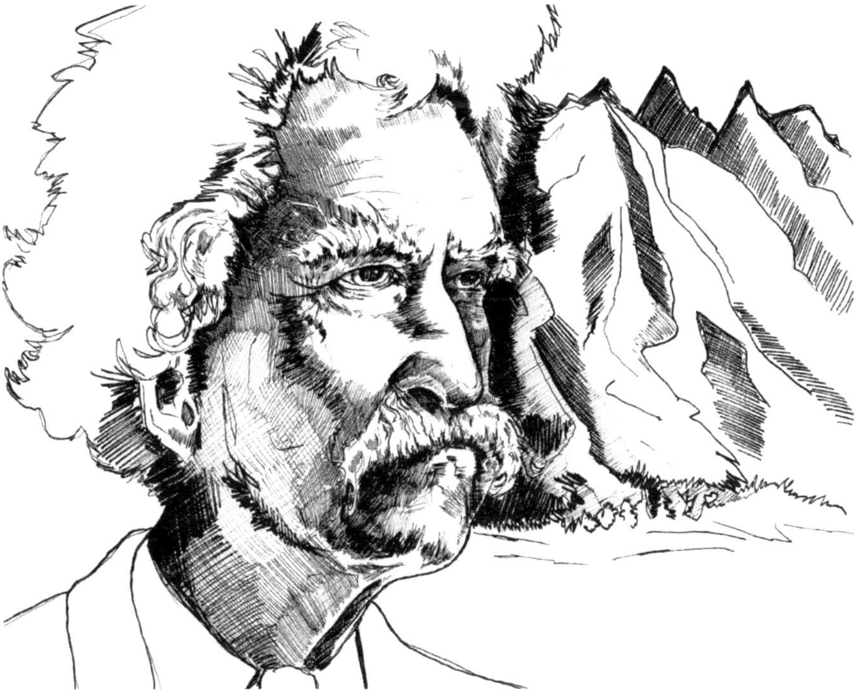

He chose as topics to satirize everything from Mormonism's sacred experiences to its perceived peculiarities and social experiences.

The cynical tone of his article about "Valley Tan," an alleged heavy-handed drink used among Utah's early pioneer residents, is obvious in the following passage from an entry by Twain that appeared in his book *Roughing It*: "Valley tan (or, at least, one form of valley tan) is a kind of whisky, or first cousin to it; is of Mormon invention and manufactured only in Utah. Tradition says it is made of (imported) fire and brimstone. If I remember rightly no public drinking saloons were allowed in the kingdom by Brigham Young, and no private drinking permitted among the faithful, except they confined themselves to 'valley tan.'"

Made from "fire and brimstone." Good one, Mr. Clemens. Twain ratcheted up the humor in his thoughts about polygamy and its uncomely looking wives:

> *Our stay in Salt Lake City amounted to only two days, and therefore we had no time to the customary inquisition into the workings of polygamy and get up the usual statistics and deductions preparatory to calling the attention of the nation at large once more to the matter. I had the will to do it. With the gushing self-sufficiency of youth I was feverish to plunge in headlong and achieve a great reform here—until I saw the Mormon women. Then I was touched. My heart was wiser than my head. It warmed toward these poor, ungainly and pathetically "homely" creatures, and as I turned to hide the generous moisture in my eyes, I said, "No—the man that marries one of them has done an act of Christian charity which entitles him to the kindly applause of mankind, not their harsh censure—and the man that marries sixty of them has done a deed of open-handed generosity so sublime that the nations should stand uncovered in his presence and worship in silence."*

If you've seen any old images of the stern-looking polygamous women, you might agree with Twain's assessment on this account. They are perhaps "ungainly" and "homely," but they also were brave and must have garnered their uncomely appearance by the trials of the times. Twain writes with humor, satire and rudeness, and sometimes you can't help but chuckle.

Twain also wrote that during his visit to Salt Lake City, he went to see Brigham Young—or, as he calls him in his book, "the king." The writer, who tried to get Young's attention, obviously wasn't impressed:

> *The second day, we made the acquaintance of Mr. Street (since deceased) and put on white shirts and went and paid a state visit to the king. He seemed a quiet, kindly, easy-mannered, dignified, self-possessed old gentleman of fifty-five or sixty, and had a gentle craft in his eye that probably belonged there. He was very simply dressed and was just taking off a straw hat as we entered. He talked about Utah, and the Indians, and Nevada, and general American matters and questions, with our secretary and certain government officials who came with us. But he never paid any attention to me, notwithstanding I made several attempts to "draw him out" on federal politics and his high handed attitude toward Congress. I thought some of the things I said were rather fine. But he merely looked around at me, at distant intervals, something as I have seen a benignant old cat look around to see which kitten was meddling with her tail.*
>
> *By and by I subsided into an indignant silence, and so sat until the end, hot and flushed, and execrating him in my heart for an ignorant savage. But he was calm. His conversation with those gentlemen flowed on as sweetly and peacefully and musically as any summer brook. When the audience was ended and we were retiring from the presence, he put his hand on my head, beamed down on me in an admiring way and said to my brother: "Ah—your child, I presume? Boy, or girl?"*

His dislike for the Mormon leader increased after this episode, which, according to *Salt Lake Tribune* writer Pat Bagley, is probably one of Twain's stretched truths since Young and the writer were the same height. Young's purported question so insulted Twain that he left Salt Lake with a bad taste in his mouth for the church leader, which may have fueled his intent to diminish the Mormons in print. Later, he wrote about the fictitious seven-foot-long, ninety-six-foot-wide bed Young used to accommodate his many wives.

In a show of contradiction, Twain said that before leaving the city, he and his brother were "hearty and well fed and happy," even "physically superb," according to Bagley's article, which hardly seems the picture of dining with an awkward and ignorant people. But Twain was making a name for himself as a satirist, and so he bumbled the stories with flavor. He also profited from his approach.

"When all is said and done," wrote Kathryn Jenkins Gordon in her insightful and amusing book *Colorful Characters in Mormon History*, "Twain earned a *lot* of money from his writings and lectures, and the ones about Mormons were wildly popular all over the world."

Part II

Spiritual Moments

From ancient prophets wandering Utah's backcountry to heaven-inspired visions from the leading brethren of the LDS Church, this section shares several spiritual moments in Utah and Mormon history. Some of the stories may be familiar to members of the LDS Church, but they are likely little known among the more general readership, thus their inclusion in a book about forgotten tales. The spiritual history of the church is part of what makes the Mormon faith so interesting. Such impressions are not easily forgotten by those who've experienced them, and they are oft remembered by those who read or hear about them later.

Moroni Visits Utah

If you're a member of the LDS faith, familiar with Mormon history or have ever read the Book of Mormon, then you're familiar with the name Moroni—a prominent figure in the Book of Mormon and Latter-day Saint history. And if you do know this man, maybe you've wondered the same thing I have: What kind of shoes did he wear?

Moroni was a wanderer, having traveled thousands of miles to escape his enemies after he saw the annihilation of his countrymen. During his sojourn, the Book of Mormon prophet, who lived some four hundred years after Christ, apparently traveled through what today is known as Utah, dedicating sites for the Lord's latter-day work. You would hope he'd had decent footwear.

The Wandering Prophet

Whether you're Mormon or not, you've probably seen Moroni around town—err, at least if you've ever turned your eyes to the gold figure that tops most LDS temples. It represents the angel that a young Joseph Smith claimed visited him multiple times on a September night in 1823, prior to him receiving the plates from which he translated the Book of Mormon.

Formerly—as in some 1,400 years before Smith—Moroni was a historian and prophet who, after his father, Mormon, died in war with the factious Lamanites, kept the Book of Mormon plates. After witnessing the demise of his nation 400 years after Christ, and after traveling on foot for perhaps 36 years from present-day Central America to New York, according to information postulated in an article by Douglas K. Christensen on *Book of Mormon Archaeology Forum*, all of that time keeping the plates in his charge, Moroni buried the record in a hill called Cumorah and prayed that one day they might be revealed anew.

For our intents and purposes, this is where our story begins. The topography of the Book of Mormon has been a matter of speculation and friendly debate in Mormon circles, but the consensus seems to be that the majority of the episodes recorded in the sacred book took place in lands south of the United States, the land where Moroni lived and with which he was familiar. We know through the reading of his account that he wandered the land, fleeing his enemies because of the war-torn age in which he lived. He wrote in Moroni 1:1–4:

> *Now I, Moroni, after having made an end of abridging the account of the people of Jared, I had supposed not to have written more, but I have not as yet perished; and I make not myself known to the Lamanites lest they should destroy me. For behold, their wars are exceedingly fierce among themselves; and because of their hatred they put to death every Nephite that will not deny the Christ. And I, Moroni, will not deny the Christ; wherefore, I wander whithersoever I can for the safety of mine own life. Wherefore, I write a few more things, contrary to that which I had supposed; for I had supposed not to have written any more; but I write a few more things, that perhaps they may be of worth unto my brethren, the Lamanites, in some future day, according to the will of the Lord.*

Eventually, Moroni wound up in what today is known as New York. It was here, on a hill that likely resembled one of his homeland (for he gave it the same name of Cumorah), where he offered a prayer and buried the record that would eventually be published to the world as the Book of Mormon, named after Moroni's father, Mormon, who was the principal caretaker of the plates before he gave them to his son. Once in Moroni's possession, he abridged the book of Ether and added his own account in the last of the volume's fifteen "books" before he buried the plates.

Dedicating Lands

Twenty-eight years after the pioneers arrived in the Great Basin, and twenty-two years after work commenced on the Salt Lake Temple, Brigham Young announced that another temple would be built in Utah. The chosen site, he said on June 25, 1875, was on a twenty-seven-acre hill near the Manti Stone Quarry. President Young apparently had some divine help selecting the location.

After construction had been delayed for nearly two years, the Prophet, while visiting the site in Sanpete County on April 25, 1877, climbed the hill with Warren S. Snow, a brother in the church, and proclaimed that the future temple's location was chosen long before the pioneers arrived and that building this House of the Lord couldn't wait any longer. The time was now. "Here is the spot where the prophet Moroni stood and dedicated this piece of land for a Temple site," President Young is reported to have told Brother Snow. As quoted in H. Donl Peterson's *Moroni: Ancient Prophet, Modern Messenger*, the Prophet further explained, "And that is the reason why the location is made here, and we can't move it from this spot; and if you and I are the only persons that come here at high noon today, we will dedicate this ground."

Work commenced on the sandstone structure shortly thereafter, and the temple was completed in May 1888. During its dedication, Orson F. Whitney, an early apostle of the restored church, claimed to have had a spiritual experience. "While sitting with my wife Zina in the midst of the congregation," he wrote, "I distinctly heard strains of music in the air about our heads. I supposed it to be from a band playing in the town; but was afterwards told by President Anthony H. Lund and others that no band was out that day. The conclusion was irresistible that the music had a heavenly source." Many others in attendance heard similar strains of music.

According to these stories, Moroni had dedicated the site for the temple, Brigham Young had brought its construction to fruition and the Lord accepted its dedication. It is alleged in LDS history that Moroni also dedicated other sites in Utah and elsewhere for temple construction, including St. George; Kirtland, Missouri; Independence, Missouri; and Nauvoo, Illinois. Perhaps he rode a pack animal for at least part of his journey, and according to hypotheses in Christensen's article, he probably didn't travel alone. There's no doubt that Moroni walked plenty over those thirty-six years before arriving at Cumorah. It's been said that nothing worthwhile is accomplished without faith and hard work. Moroni, one of the all-time great leaders in the scriptural record, had both faith and stamina. He had plenty of faith in the Lord and his promises, he worked tremendously hard to do his part in making prophecy come to pass and he wore out his shoes in that service. Let's just hope they were comfortable shoes.

FOUNDING SPIRITS

The following is a popular story in Mormon lore, but it may not be as well known among Utah's non-LDS residents. It has to do with the fourth president of the Church of Jesus Christ of Latter-day Saints, the St. George Temple and the Founding Fathers.

The American Patriots

The Latter-day Saints are a patriotic people who think highly of traditional America. Their scriptures speak of America as "a chosen land, highly favored of the Lord," in which he raised up our constitutional fathers "for this very purpose" of establishing the foundational freedoms of the land. Latter-day Saints believe that the U.S. Constitution is a divinely decreed and inspired document and that the framers and founders of it were God-fearing men who were led by the Lord to do the work they did. They believe that Columbus's rediscovery of the New World, America's break with Great Britain, the War of 1776, the Declaration of Independence and said Constitution were all part of divine preparation of bringing religious freedom to a time and place in which a greater work could happen—namely, the restoration of the gospel of Jesus Christ in the form of a church bearing his name.

Mormons also believe that America, specifically within the borders of the United States, will be home to the future New Jerusalem, a city prophesied in scripture where Christ will rule during a millennial era of peace and prosperity during his second advent. America is God's chosen land for his latter-day work, according to LDS teachings, and even though it must pass through trial and tribulation, it has a glorious future. America's Founding Fathers were not perfect men, but the Lord used them to do a great work. As such, they are highly revered by the Mormons. According to Wilford Woodruff, these same men wanted to be baptized in the Mormon faith; they just didn't know it at the time because the church was not yet organized in their day. But they let Brother Woodruff know later on.

The Great Record Keeper

Wilford Woodruff is among the more memorable characters in Mormon history. Even his name, which can be a bit of a tongue twister for some communicators, is difficult to forget. What makes him important in LDS and Utah history, besides being an apostle and becoming the fourth president of the church, are his journals. Woodruff kept a daily journal from shortly after he was baptized at age twenty-six on December 31, 1833, until near the end of his life on September 2, 1898. He recorded episodes of the early church—some that are not found anywhere else. His meticulous habit spanned more than sixty years and many separate volumes. Woodruff ascribed journal keeping as a necessary and fulfilling duty.

"From the outset, his journal reflected a sense of destiny," wrote Francis Gibbons in his biography *Wilford Woodruff: Wondrous Worker, Prophet of God.* "Following the title page appears the caption 'The First Book of Wilford' and this opening statement: 'When in the course of human events has there ever been a more important period than at the present day and age of the world?' He then defined the twofold purpose of his journal: 'first, to provide a measuring stick by which his life could be evaluated'; and second, to fulfill a 'duty to keep an accurate account of our proceedings.'"

Gibbons, who has written several biographies of the modern prophets, continued his analysis of the great journal writer:

> *Later, in an article he wrote for the* Juvenile Instructor, *Elder Woodruff elaborated on his concept of the proper content and value of a journal. "What shall I write?" he asked rhetorically. "Write about anything that is worth preserving," he answered. He then ascribed the existence of the holy scriptures to the work of selfless, nameless journalists. "If men had not kept*

> *a journal in former days," wrote Wilford, "we should not now have any Bible, Book of Mormon, Doctrine and Covenants or any other book."...As to the personal satisfaction to be derived from a journal, he wrote: "I have kept a journal for forty years, and it is now a great pleasure to me and my family to sit down and read an account of our travels, where we have been, and what we have done, and the dealings of God with us, and the many good times we have had with our friends." He also mentioned the pleasure of reviewing "the good teachings" of the leaders of the Church that he had taken the pains to record, sometimes verbatim.*

In his journals are recorded everything from the mundane to the extraordinary, from meeting schedules and the day's weather to doctrinal teachings from the early brethren and remarkable spiritual experiences, some of them not his own. One of the more memorable experiences not only affected President Woodruff but also had a significant impact on the church. It was a vision that helped cement the importance of temple work for the Latter-day Saints and those who have their eyes on us from beyond the veil.

Why Baptize for the Dead?

In First Corinthians 15:29, the Apostle Paul asked the question, "Else what shall they do which are baptized for the dead, if the dead rise not at all? why are they then baptized for the dead?" Mormons say they have the answer.

Paul was teaching of the resurrection. In essence, he asked why baptism was performed for the deceased if those performing it did not believe in a future resurrection. Why then baptize for the dead if there won't be any resurrection? Why go to all the trouble?

Paul knew that the future resurrection of men and women, made possible because of Jesus Christ's atonement, would one day happen. He obviously also knew of the practice of baptizing for the dead, otherwise he wouldn't have mentioned it.

Mormons believe that God meant what he said: all men and women must be baptized by water and of the Spirit in order to be eligible to inherit the Kingdom of God. Even Christ, who is perfect, submitted to baptism because it was a commandment from his father. But not all men and women have the opportunity to learn of Jesus Christ and his gospel and accept baptism in the flesh before they die. What happens then?

If all are to one day stand before God to be judged on equal terms, Mormons believe, then all persons living and dead must have the same opportunity of hearing the gospel message and either accepting it or rejecting it. The LDS practice of baptizing for the deceased gives our ancestors this equal footing. The deceased do not have to accept what has been done for them, but it is offered in love as an opportunity if they so wish to accept it.

Apparently, according to the following testimony by Wilford Woodruff, the spirits of America's Founding Fathers wanted this opportunity.

Wilford's Remarkable Vision

Wilford Woodruff claimed that on August 21, 1877, the spirits of George Washington, Thomas Jefferson and other early American Patriots visited him while he was inside the St. George Temple, an elegant white sandstone building that stands stately against the red lava rock of St. George. According to Woodruff, these spirits wanted to know why the church had not yet done proxy baptism for them. The twenty-six-volume *Journal of Discourses*, which contains hundreds of sermons and other teachings from the early church leaders, records Woodruff's testimony (in volume 19):

> *I will here say, before closing, that two weeks before I left St. George, the spirits of the dead gathered around me, wanting to know why we did not redeem them. Said they, "Have you had the use of the Endowment House for a number of years, and yet nothing has ever been done for us. We laid the foundation of the government you now enjoy, and we never apostatized from it, but we remained true to it and were faithful to God." These were the signers of the Declaration of Independence, and they waited on me for two days and two nights. I thought it very singular, that notwithstanding so much work had been done, and yet nothing had been done for them. The thought never entered my heart, from the fact, I suppose, that heretofore our minds were reaching after our more immediate friends and relatives. I straightway went into the baptismal font* [in the temple] *and called upon brother* [John] *McCallister to baptize me for the signers of the Declaration of Independence, and fifty other eminent men, making one hundred in all, including John Wesley, Columbus, and others.*

"It was a very interesting day," Woodruff wrote in his journal for that date. "I felt thankful that we had the privilege and the power to administer for the worthy dead, especially for the signers of the Declaration of Independence, that inasmuch as they laid the foundation of our government, that we could do as much for them as they had done for us."

A Vision

Wilford Woodruff, a true visionary in the most literal sense of the word, was a meticulous journal writer. If it weren't for his careful hand, much of LDS history would be unknown. Scattered among the historic gems he put to paper are spiritual experiences, mostly his own, but sometimes of others so gifted.

Wilford titled the following account simply "A Vision," not giving it any attribution. It has long been believed by some to perhaps be a dream given to Woodruff's predecessor, President John Taylor, third president of the LDS Church. But this raises a question: Why did Woodruff record the dream and not Taylor or his secretary, George Reynolds, who recorded President Taylor's many other revelations as the prophet dictated them?

Authors Richard Neitzel Holzapfel and Christopher C. Jones explained it this way: "Today, copies of John Taylor's written revelations are found in the journals of Church leaders and lay members who treasured the words of the Lord when they recorded them in their private records."

Whether it was Taylor's dream or Woodruff's perhaps is not as important as the account itself. It is not a pleasant entry, and it is quite graphic in its depictions of a last days scenario. It mentions Utah, and it is interesting because of the millennial fervor it depicts. Early church leaders often taught that the Second Coming of Christ was just around the corner, but before that time arrived, society would sink to the brink of despair. The following entry, which may be familiar to some members of the church but likely not to the general reader, is a bit lengthy but is included here in its entirety. Woodruff dated the entry June 15, 1878, and listed it simply as "A Vision, Salt Lake City, Night of Dec 16, 1877."

> *I went to bed as usual at about 7:30 PM. I had been reading a revelation in the French language. My mind was calm, more so than usual if possible, so I composed myself for sleep, but could not. I felt a strange feeling come over me and apparently became partially unconscious. Still I was not asleep, nor exactly awake, with dreary feeling. The first thing that I recognized was*

that I was in the tabernacle of Ogden, Utah. I was sitting in the back part of the building for fear they would call on me to preach, which however they did, for after singing the second time they called me to the stand.

I arose to speak and said that I didn't know that I had anything especially to say, except to bear my testimony of the Latter-day work, when all at once it seemed as if I was lifted out of myself and I said, "Yes, I have something to say and that is this: Some of my brethren have been asking, 'What is becoming of us? What is the wind blowing?' I will answer you right here what is coming very shortly."

I was then in a dream, immediately in the city of Salt Lake, and wandering around in the streets and in all parts of the city, and on the doors of the houses I found badges of mourning and I could not find a house but was in mourning. I passed my own house and found the same sign there, and I asked the question, "Is that me that is dead?" Someone gave me the answer, "No, you will get through it all."

It seemed strange to me that I saw no person in the streets in all my wandering around the country. I seemed to be in their houses with the sick, but saw no funeral procession, nor anything of the kind, but the city looking still and as though the people were praying. And it seemed that they had controlled the disease, but what the disease was I did not learn; it was not made known to me. I then looked over the country, north, east, south, and west, and the same mourning was in every land and in every place.

The next thing I knew I was just this side of Omaha. It seemed though I was above the earth, and looking down upon it. As I passed along upon my way east I saw the road full of people, mostly women, with just what they could carry in bundles on their backs, traveling to the mountains on foot. I wondered how they would get through with such a small pack on their backs. It was remarkable to us that there were so few men among them. It didn't seem to me as though the cars were running, the rails looked rusty and the roads abandoned; and I have no conception of how I traveled as I looked down upon the people.

I continued east by the way of Omaha and Council Bluffs, which were full of disease. There were women everywhere. The state of Illinois and Missouri were in a tumult, men killing one another, women joining the fighting, family against family in the most horrid manner.

I imagined next that I was in Washington and I found desolation there. The White House was empty and the Halls of Congress the same, and everything in ruins. The people seemed to have left the city and left it to take care of itself.

I was in Baltimore. In the square where the Monument of 1812 stands in front of the Charles Hotel. I saw dead piled up so as to fill the street square. I saw mothers cutting the throats of their own children for their blood. I saw them suck it from their throats to quench their own thirst and then lie down and die. The water of Chesapeake Bay was stagnant, and the stench arising from it on account of their throwing their bodies into it so terrible, that the very smell carried death with it. I saw no man except they were dead or dying in the streets and very few women. Those I saw were crazy and in an ugly condition. Everywhere I went I beheld the same sights all over the city; it was terrible beyond description to look upon.

I thought this must be the end; but no, I was seemingly in an instant in the city of Philadelphia. There everything was still. No living soul was there to greet me. It seemed the whole city was without any inhabitants. In the south of Chestnut Street and in fact everywhere I went, the putrefaction of the dead caused such a stench that it was impossible for any living thing to breathe, nor did I see any living thing in the city.

Next I found myself in Broadway, in the city of New York, and there it seemed the people had done the best they could to overcome the disease, but in wandering down Broadway I saw the bodies of beautiful women lying, some dead and others in a dying condition, on the sidewalks. I saw men come out of cellars and ravish the persons of some that were yet alive and then kill them and rob their bodies of all the valuables they had upon them. Then before they could get back to the cellar they would roll over a time or two and die in agony. In some of the back streets I saw them kill some of their own offspring and eat their raw flesh, and in a few minutes die themselves. Everywhere I went I saw the same scene of horror and destruction and death and rapine.

No carriages, buggies, or cars were running; but death and destruction were everywhere. Then I saw fire start and just at that moment a mighty East wind sprang up and carried the flames over the city and it burned until there was not a single building left standing there, even down to the waters edge. Wharves and shipping all seemed to burn and follow in common destruction where the "great city" was a short time ago. The stench from the bodies that were burning was so great that it was carried a long distance cross the Hudson Bay and carried death and destruction wherever it penetrated. I cannot paint in words the horror that seemed to compass me about; it was beyond description of man.

I supposed this was the end; but it was not. I was given to understand the same horror was being enacted all over the country, east, west, north, and south. Few were left alive, still there were some.

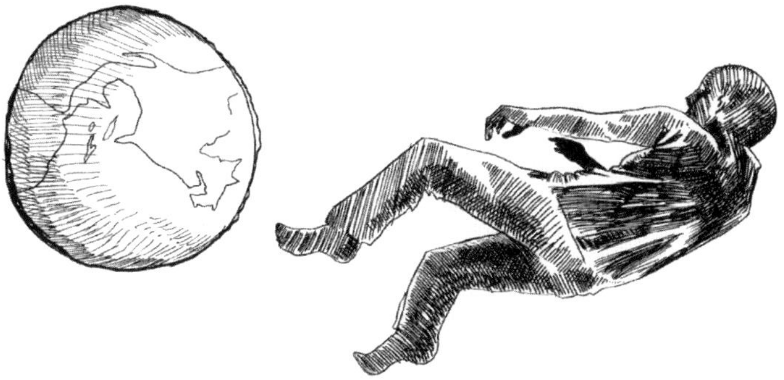

Immediately after I seemed to be standing on the left bank of the Missouri River, opposite the City of Independence, but there was no city. I saw the whole state of Missouri and Illinois and all of Iowa, a complete desert with no living being there. A short distance from the river however, I saw twelve men dressed in temple robes, standing in a square or nearly so (and I understood it represented the Twelve Gates of the New Jerusalem). Their hands were uplifted in consecration of the ground and laying the corner stone of the temple. I saw myriads of angels hovering over them, and saw also an immense pillar of clouds over them and heard the angels singing the most heavenly music. The words were "Now is established the Kingdom of God and his Christ, which shall never more be thrown down."

I saw people coming from the river and from the desert places a long way off to help build the temple and it seemed that hosts of angels all helped to get material to build with and I saw some of them who wore temple clothes come and build the temple and the city, and all the time I saw the great pillar of clouds hovering over the place.

Instantly, however, I found myself again in the tabernacle at Ogden. And yet, I could still see the building go on and I got quite animated in calling on the people in the tabernacle to listen to the beautiful music, for the angels were singing the same music I had heard before. "Now is established the Kingdom of God and his Christ, which shall never more be thrown down."

At this I seemed to stagger back from the pulpit and Brother Francis D. Richards and some others caught my arm and prevented me from falling. Then I finished so abruptly. Still even then I had not fainted, but was simply exhausted.

Then I rolled over in bed and awoke just as the city clock was striking twelve.

A Prophecy of the Vernal Temple

While at the dedication of the Uintah Stake Tabernacle on August 24, 1907, LDS Church president Joseph F. Smith said that he "would not be surprised if the day would come when a temple would be built in your own midst here." His words proved prophetic some ninety years later, when in November 1997 the Vernal Utah Temple was dedicated by President Gordon B. Hinckley. The old tabernacle, which was the site of many church and community functions over the decades, was itself turned into a modern House of the Lord.

It was the tenth temple built in Utah and the first temple built from an existing building. "A modern temple was built within the shell of the gutted tabernacle, which had fallen into serious disrepair and had not hosted a stake conference since 1983," reads an entry on LDS.org. "The idea of converting the Uintah Stake Tabernacle into the Vernal Utah Temple was first proposed by leaders of the Vernal Utah Glines Stake to area authorities in 1984, but the proposal was eventually rejected by the First Presidency," the website reads. "Many other possibilities were pursued, and the building had even been put up for sale for a time. However, in 1993, the idea of a temple was proposed again. This time, it met with First Presidency approval."

Before it closed as a tabernacle, more than 18,000 visitors toured the site, bespeaking the influence it had on the community over the years. Later, when it opened for a public open house before its dedication as a temple, the site received some 118,700 visitors.

Here are a few interesting items about this tabernacle turned temple: "All of the furniture and fixtures salvaged from the Uintah Stake Tabernacle were sold at public auction on April 15, 1995. Everything available sold in 3½ hours." Also, "the old dome of the Uintah Stake Tabernacle was removed and renovated into a gazebo, located at the Ashley Valley Community Park. The Vernal Utah Temple was given two domes instead of one, as was featured on the tabernacle."

The Devil Comes to Logan

Logan, today a busy city in northern Utah's pretty Cache Valley, isn't that different from other places named after an early resident or town founder. In Logan's case, the city was named in 1860 after fur trapper Ephraim Logan. A group of Mormon settlers founded the area after Brigham Young sent them north to colonize the land. He sent settlers to other points across the territory, including south to the St. George area. The church in both places—St. George and Logan—eventually built temples.

One of the more interesting stories in Mormon lore is of the Logan Temple. Unlike the other spiritual-focused stories in this section, this one is a bit darker. It concerns an alleged visit that old Mr. Scratch himself made to the Logan Temple in the early 1890s.

Dedicated between May 17 and 19, 1884, the Logan Temple was the second temple completed in Utah. The devil's attempt to storm the temple with a malicious army of spirits is shared in Nolan P. Olsen's memorable history, *The Logan Temple: The First 100 Years*.

The devil's visit to the temple occurred while temple president Marriner W. Merrill was in his office one morning. As the story goes, he heard a commotion outside the building. When he went to look out the window to see where the ruckus was coming from, he noticed a "great congregation of people coming up the temple hill, some on foot, and others on horseback and in carriages."

Were these Latter-day Saints who had come to do ordinance work in the temple? And if so, he wondered, how will we accommodate so many people? Taking another look at the approaching throng, however, he noticed that they did not look like your normal temple-going folk. He soon received the answer to his questions. The crowd had not come to do acts of Christian charity in the Lord's house but rather to thwart the work from progressing.

After tying up their horses "at the hitching posts, or by turning them loose on the temple corrals," the men walked about the grounds but made no effort to enter the building. "They were rather an off looking group, and were dressed quite shabbily." President Merrill, determined to find out why the men had come to the temple, went out to inquire about their visit. The leader of the group answered, "I am Satan, and these are my people."

President Merrill, who stood his ground instead of retreating to safety inside the sacred building, then asked for what purpose the devil and his minions had come. "I don't like what is being done in the Logan Temple and have come to stop it," the devil replied.

Olsen shared the rest of the story in his reverent and interesting book:

> *That was a bit of a shock to President Merrill, and he answered: "No, we will not stop it. This is the work of the Lord and must go on. You know that you or any one else can not stop the work of the Lord."*

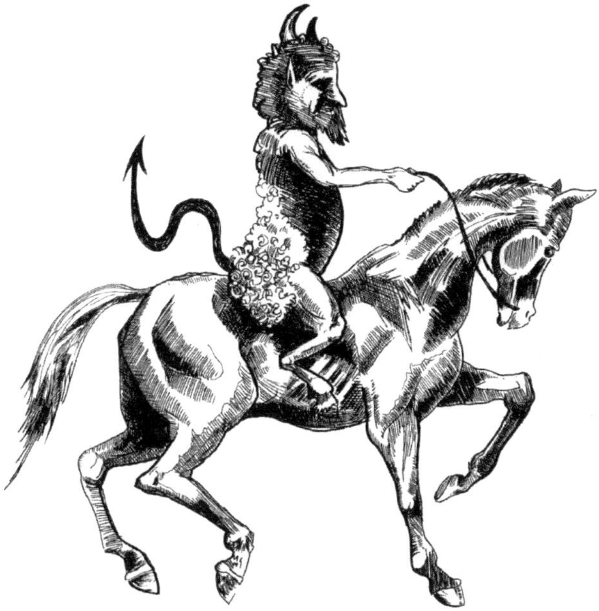

> *"If you refuse to stop it, I will tell you what I propose to do," the adversary said. "I will scatter this congregation of people throughout these valleys, and we will keep people from coming to the temple. We will whisper in their ears and discourage them from attending the temple. This will stop your temple work."*
>
> *President Merrill then used the power of his priesthood and commanded Satan and his followers to depart from holy ground. He said that within four or five minutes there was not a person, horse or buggy in sight. They just disappeared into thin air and were gone.*

Some readers, maybe even modern members of the LDS Church, may find this story difficult to believe, perhaps considering it one of the religion's fables. Although it is a unique story, its validity is not out of the realm of possibility for faithful Mormons. The church is built on supernatural occurrences, starting with Joseph Smith's vision of 1820. Latter-day Saints verily believe in the literal existence of a loving God and his Son, Jesus Christ, but they also believe in the reality of Satan and his influence in a sin-soaked world. They believe Satan's chief aim is to thwart the work of God and make all humankind miserable like unto himself. And to the faithful Mormon, the temple is where much of God's work takes place, so why wouldn't the devil and his minions try to stop that work from progressing, even if it required them to appear as rough riders on horseback?

Still, the story does lend itself to speculation. For instance, Mormons believe the Bible. It is recorded in Revelation 12:7–9 that "there was war in heaven: Michael and his angels fought against the dragon; and the dragon fought and his angels, And prevailed not; neither was their place found any more in heaven. And the great dragon was cast out, that old serpent, called the Devil, and Satan, which deceiveth the whole world: he was cast out into the earth, and his angels were cast out with him." According to this, Latter-day Saints believe that Satan is on the earth but without a physical body. Rather, he is a fallen angel, one of spirit substance and not flesh and bone. So how did he appear to President Merrill as a physical being riding a horse?

President Charles W. Penrose, an apostle in the early 1900s, explained that on many occasions throughout the world's history, Satan has appeared to select individuals as an "angel of light" to try to deceive and lead them astray. He appeared to Joseph Smith, Moses and even Jesus Christ, but he failed in his attempts to sway them. And if this story is true, he also appeared to the early president of the Logan Temple.

As for the message that the devil and his minions left with President Merrill on the day he came to Logan, perhaps he hasn't failed so completely. If you're a Latter-day Saint who hasn't been to the temple in a while, maybe, as that fallen angel of light warned on the temple hill that day long ago, he has whispered in your ear and discouraged you from attending the House of the Lord. If so, you should find solace in another belief of the Church: God is more powerful and wise than Satan, and the devil cannot stop the Lord's work from moving forward. The believing Mormon will repent, put one's best foot forward, try to overcome personal weaknesses and let the grace of Christ—through the atonement that he wrought in Gethsemane, Golgotha and before an empty tomb—work in his or her life. And in so doing, the covenant Mormon will make the temple the pinnacle of his or her worship and beat back the powers of the adversary.

President George Q. Cannon, another early apostle, said as he spoke of the Logan Temple on November 12, 1877, "Every foundation stone that is laid for a Temple, and every Temple completed according to the order the Lord has revealed for his holy Priesthood, lessens the power of Satan on the earth, and increases the power of God and Godliness, moves the heavens in mighty power in our behalf, invokes and calls down upon us the blessings of the Eternal Gods, and those who reside in their presence." These are not tall tales—nor are they nearly forgotten—for most Latter-day Saints.

Part III
Ancient Land

When the pioneers arrived in the Great Basin in the summer of 1847, it was a monumental moment in LDS Church and American history, one that helped shape the territory and Utah's history. But long before the pioneers arrived with their handcarts and covered wagons, many other people had lived and roamed and made the region their home. These people from many Indian tribes left their marks in the sandstone rocks and prairies and add a deeper layer to the history that is Utah. Of course, there also are the giant behemoths of the Jurassic Period that left something of themselves behind. They have their own tales to tell in the rock beds, such as those in northeast Utah.

Dinosaur Tracks

From head to tail it was about twenty feet in length and weighed some 1,100 pounds. But its size didn't keep the Dilophosaurus from moving quickly across the red sand and green forested landscape. Its two hind legs moved quickly because a much larger dinosaur, also a bipedal predator, was in pursuit.

Allosaurus, more than thirty feet long and weighing some three thousand pounds, gnashed its massive teeth and clenched its vicious claws as it pursued its prey across the arid landscape. Lightning danced in the darkening sky as thunder boomed overhead. The rain would come next.

The Dilophosaurus cut through a thick forest, slowing its pursuer, which could not maneuver the trees as well as its smaller, more efficient prey. Just as the Dilophosaurus exited the trees, it felt the first drops of rain. The red sand of the landscape turned to mush as warm rain fell in torrents, causing the creature's claws to dig deep as it escaped the hunter.

The area was hills and valleys. As the Dilophosaurus reached a peak, it slowed, trying to catch its breath, and looked back to see that the Allosaurus also had slowed but had not given up the chase. The Dilophosaurus, with twin fins atop its crocodile-looking head, would have to increase the pace. The Allosaurus was not one to give up easily.

The smaller dinosaur breathed deeply but knew it'd have to keep moving if it had any chance of surviving. Perhaps if the Dilophosaurus had been in a pack, things would be different. Then, maybe, they could stand their ground against the bigger dinosaur. But it was alone, and the best option it had was to run.

The veins in the Dilophosaurus's face strained, and the creature made a screeching sound before it took off in another dash, this time down the mountain peak and into the valley floor below, its claws once more making imprints in the earth's crust—imprints that would remain for millions of years.

***

If you visit sites in the Ashley National Forest near Vernal, you can still see imprints left by Dilophosaurus in several places in this ancient land. One place is near Red Fleet Reservoir, where several dinosaur footprints are clearly visible along a rocky beachfront of the reservoir. These ancient footprints, left from the Jurassic Period some 193 million years ago, continue on a downward slope, right into the reservoir itself, attesting that this scenic area in northeastern Utah was at one time a landscape of peaks and valleys. Sadly, some of these priceless historical markers have been vandalized by uncaring and thoughtless individuals.

I had the opportunity to visit the site in early 2015, while covering the third annual Paddle Fest at the reservoir for a June 23 story I was to write for the *Vernal Express*, where I worked for a short time as the newspaper's managing editor:

> *In some family groups, while children and teens splashed in the water, mom and dad were lazily taking in sun rays on the beach. In other instances the*

scene was reversed: adults were in the water while children rested on the warm sand.

A popular recreation spot was near the boat docks, but some recreationists found enjoyment away from the crowds. Across the waves, Steve Sroka, park manager and paleontologist with the Utah Field House of Natural History State Park Museum, was giving guided tours of dinosaur tracks, many which can still be seen imprinted into the hard crust of the earth.

Most of the tracks are believed to have been from dilophosaurus or similar dinosaur, he said. The dinosaur tracks sparked the interest of Utah media, including a television station and the Vernal Express, *which were ferried to the rocky cliffs to see the pre-history imprints.*

It's a shame, Sroka said, that over the years some of the tracks have been vandalized by careless visitors.

"People just don't have any respect for historical markers," he said.

When Sroka told me the story about how a group of young people had chipped away at some of the dinosaur tracks and threw them into the reservoir, I felt disgusted that fellow human beings could have profound disrespect for such priceless natural wonders.

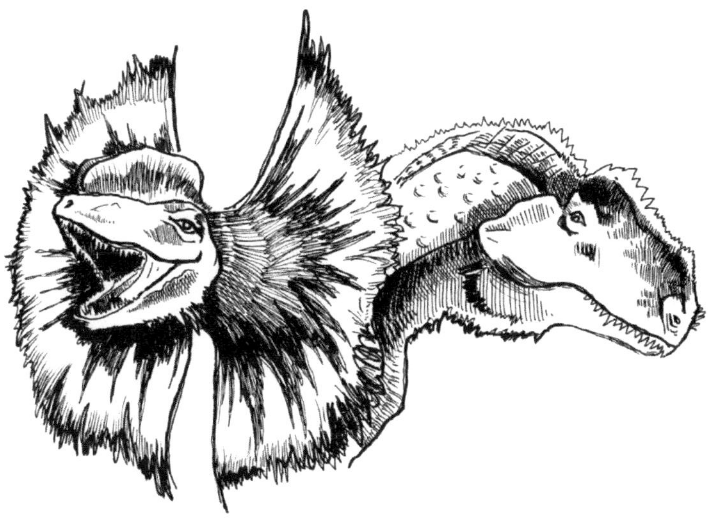

Several species of dinosaur, including the Dilophosaurus, one of the creatures depicted in the movie *Jurassic Park*, are believed to have lived in the area during the Jurassic Period. The description of the dinosaur in the fictionalized story at the beginning of this chapter is based on what paleontologists believe Dilophosaurus may have been like when it walked the earth some 65 million years ago.

As I looked over Red Fleet before leaving the Paddle Fest for the day and noticed all the people on the sandy beaches and in the water, my eyes wandered across the waves to the rocky bank, where the footprints of the Dilophosaurus remained. In the same instant, my thoughts wandered to another time and a scene I had imagined: Red Fleet didn't exist yet, and instead of people on the beaches, there were dinosaurs roaming a landscape that appeared very different than it does today. I felt more than a little blessed to know that these ancient creatures left something of themselves behind and only hoped that there would not be any other irreverent people who'd vandalize such priceless history. I walked back to my car, feeling thankful for the opportunity I had as a journalist and writer to cover what may at first have seemed a mundane and uninteresting story. Although the article was about paddle boarding and celebrating at the reservoir, I had come to know the Dilophosaurus a little better that day.

THE MYSTERIOUS ANASAZIS

Long before the Mormon pioneers arrived, parts of the place today known as Utah were once inhabited by an ancient race of people known as the Anasazis. The tale of the Anasazis is a mysterious one. It is believed that they lived in the area for some 1,300 years before disappearing. No one knows for sure what happened to this ancient and curious tribe, but it has become the stuff of legend and tall tales. Talented fiction writers have used the Anasazis as the basis for adventure and mystery stories. Popular western writer Louis L'Amour, for instance, built a suspenseful story around the Anasazis in his book *The Haunted Mesa*, a thrilling adventure novel that keeps the reader spellbound by its atmosphere and escapism. But while all novels have a conclusion to their story, the true tale of the Anasazis remains one shrouded in wonder.

The Anasazis—or "Ancient Ones," as the name means—are believed to be ancestors of the Pueblo Indians and lived in the Four Corners region

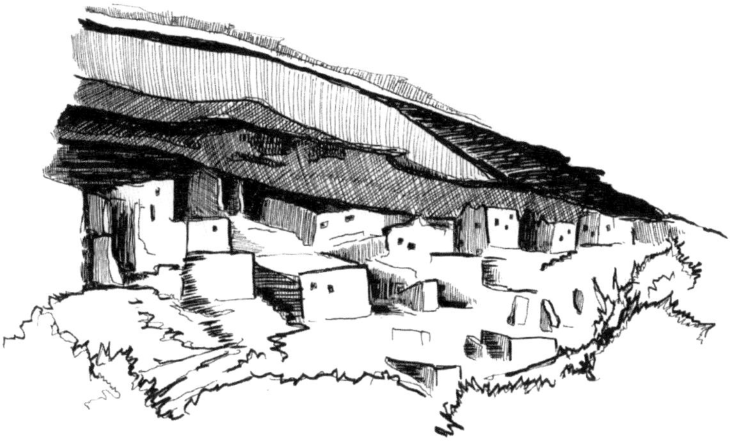

of southern Utah and Colorado and northern Arizona and New Mexico principally between the second and thirteenth centuries but perhaps rising as early as 1500 BC. In about AD 1250, according to scholar David Roberts, the tribe cut dwellings into the area's sandstone cliffs, which were discovered in the 1880s by Anglo explorers. These magnificent creations sparked the tribe's nickname, "Cliff Dwellers."

The Anasazis were an industrious, ingenious people, quite sophisticated for their time. And there were thousands of them. In a July 2003 article in the *Smithsonian Magazine*, Roberts wrote of the "30,000-square-mile landscape of canyons, buttes and mesas" as at one time being "populated by as many as 30,000 people. The Anasazis built magnificent villages such as Chaco Canyon's Pueblo Bonito [in New Mexico], a tenth-century complex that was as many as five stories tall and contained about 800 rooms. The people laid a 400-mile network of roads, some of them 30 feet wide, across deserts and canyons. And into their architecture they built sophisticated astronomical observatories."

Arizona, Colorado, New Mexico, Utah—these were all the stomping grounds of the ancient race. But then, one day, they mysteriously disappeared—or so it seemed. Like the ghost ship at sea whose staterooms and dining salons are empty except for the clothes on the beds and the dishes on the tables, the desert was deserted except for the human-hewed caves in the cliffs. What happened to the tribe?

Roberts went on to explain some possibilities of the Anasazis' disappearance:

> *Toward the end of the 13th century, some cataclysmic event forced the Anasazi to flee those cliff houses and their homeland and to move south and east toward the Rio Grande and the Little Colorado River. Just what happened has been the greatest puzzle facing archaeologists who study the ancient culture. Today's Pueblo Indians have oral histories about their peoples' migration, but the details of these stories remain closely guarded secrets. Within the past decade, however, archaeologists have wrung from the pristine ruins new understandings about why the Anasazi left, and the picture that emerges is dark. It includes violence and warfare—even cannibalism—among the Anasazi themselves. "After about A.D. 1200, something very unpleasant happens," says University of Colorado archaeologist Stephen Lekson. "The wheels come off."*

Although there is much we do not know about the Anasazis, including the reason for their disappearance, there does seem to be some consensus by scholars about what may have happened to this innovative and secretive tribe. While the conclusions don't wrap up the mystery of this ancient class of people tight and tidy like a writer does with his novel, the real-life drama that unfolded seems to make sense. Instead of supernatural forces being in play, the Anasazis' disappearance was likely the result of a combination of violence among differing factions, severe drought in the region and arriving nomads. Because their disappearance was so sudden, the mystery surrounding the Anasazis is what makes them such a colorful topic for talented story writers like L'Amour.

ANCIENT WRITINGS

The shaman stood outside the dwelling, hearing the moans of his wife inside. He knew that the woman was in great pain, but such discomfort would soon be over and for her effort she'd be blessed with a child. Boy or girl, they did not know. But they soon would. The woman's cries increased, and the elderly man raised his arms to the heavens, petitioning a blessing on the mother and her child. When he again put them down, the woman's cries had stopped. His heart leaped, and he stepped into the dwelling, dimly lit with a small fire, where a handmaiden was attending to the child. His wife's face, which appeared tired and worn, glistened with perspiration. Just a few minutes before, that face was no doubt contorted in agony as she delivered the child, but now that the ordeal was over, her face, despite its wetness, was bathed in the glow of sweet relief. She reached to the handmaiden, who finished wiping the birth fluids from the infant, and beckoned to hold her baby. The handmaiden smiled and placed the child gently in her arms. The child seemed perfect in every way. But on his left foot was a tiny sixth toe. No matter—the child was destined for great things. It was an omen, a sign from the Great Spirit. The extra toe added to his uniqueness. The shaman, who also was the boy's father, again raised his hands to the heavens, thanking the Great One for this gift. After meeting his child and reassuring his wife, he went to the rock wall of the cave. Taking an emblem from a leather sack draped about his loins, he began to record the special moment on the rock's surface. As the images took shape, a thought came into his mind: "I wonder who, when we are gone from this place, will see my drawing. And will they know what it means?" And then, just like that, his son let out a squeal, and his thoughts about the future readers of his work were gone. They were back on his own time and place, inside the cave that he and his growing family called home.

***

Since our earliest days, mankind has communicated through not only spoken words but also written words and even drawings. Such historical emblems have been found in old parchments and plates or engraved in hard rock. Some left their marks as human beings just to say that they were here, once upon a time, on Earth. Others left histories of their people, both secular and religious. All of them are stories. We can only wonder what these ancients would have thought if they could have seen our computer-driven world today. Better yet, what do we think of the writings and drawings they left us on the tools they used in their day (parchment, golden plates and stone)?

The inscriptions on Newspaper Rock State Historic Monument, a two-hundred-square-foot rock located near Canyonlands National Park in southeastern Utah, date back some 1,500 years. It is one of the best-preserved sites of ancient inscriptions in the Southwest. Unlike modern newsprint, which is filled with descriptive words and complemented by photographs, these ancient rock drawings—petroglyphs—are all about the visual form. If you were a child of the times, the wall perhaps would read like a storybook.

The dense drawings include pictures of people, animals and symbols, most of which are unknown or mysterious. And there are drawings of people with six-toed feet. Those who left their mark here were many, from several different Native American cultures, including the Anasazi, Fremont and Navajo tribes.

Several other places in Utah are decorated with the writings and symbolisms of the Fremont Indians, such as the petroglyphs and pictoglyphs on the red rock walls in parts of Dinosaur National Monument near Vernal. These images of figures, lizards, birds and other animals and symbols are believed to have been carved many hundreds of years ago. Many of the ancient carvings and paintings are easily accessible on self-guided tours of the monument. Their meanings, and why they were created in the first place, seem to be lost to the current generation, but it is nonetheless exciting to see messages from a people who lived so long ago. We cannot help but ask, "What are you trying to tell us?"

"Why did the Fremont create these designs and what did they mean?" reads information on the National Park Service website about the ancient artwork. "Perhaps the designs served some ceremonial or religious purpose, related to hunting activities, identified clans, or simply expressed the artist's imagination—or perhaps all or none of these. Attempts to interpret the designs by comparing them with recent Native American groups may provide clues, but the true meaning remains a mystery."

Part IV

Controversies, Conflicts and Living in the West

The desert West wasn't all sagebrush and brown. It was colored by the many different characters who painted interesting stories of Utah by their quirks, secrets and feuds. One of the more colorful characters who makes up this section is Josie Basset Morris, a determined and self-reliant woman who lived alone in a cozy cabin in the rough wilds of nature (for fifty years!). There's also that colorful outlaw known as Butch Cassidy, but his real name was Robert Parker. You'll also briefly meet Thomas Rhoades before journeying alongside Chief Wakara to the fabled Spanish mines of the Uinta Mountains. There's more, of course, such as a few ornery newspaper editors.

Hidden Treasure

Thoughts of riches have haunted the dreams of countless people over the centuries. Some seek long and hard to obtain their worldly treasures, while others seek but do not seem to find. A few people fall into luck without much forethought or planning. A man by the name of Thomas Rhoades seems to fit this last category, but his story takes an interesting turn.

For our purposes, his story begins in 1846, when Brigham Young sent him on an exploratory mission to lands west of the Rocky Mountains. He went farther than he intended and wound up in California—at just the right time and place to secure his worldly riches. Rhoades, instead of returning to report his find to Brigham Young, decided to stay in California and secured a job working for John Sutter, who laid claim to a mine like many people who came to California in search of their riches. It seemed to be an ingenious move on Rhoades's part, for just three years later, Sutter's mill struck gold. By this time, the Latter-day Saints had settled in the Great Basin. Filling his pocketbook, Rhoades eventually traveled to Utah at the request of Brigham Young. The church president had another mission for Rhoades.

There was rumor of a Spanish mine that only the Ute Indians knew about and was allegedly filled with gold, jewelry and other treasures from the 1776 explorations of two Spanish priests, Francisco Dominguez and Silvestre de Escalante. On their way from New Mexico to Colorado, they traveled through parts of Utah, allegedly with the treasures in their possession, which they hid in secretive caves somewhere in the Uinta Mountains—a place later known only to the Ute Indians. Or so the story goes.

It was Chief Wakara, who had friendly relationships with the Mormons, who agreed to show Rhoades the lost cave of the Spanish treasure, but on one condition: Rhoades had to promise that any treasure he took from the mine would only be used for church purposes, not for personal gain or profit. Rhoades agreed to the terms, and in 1852, the old Indian chief led him into the mountains, the first of several trips he'd make over the next three years, taking the cave's riches piecemeal. Later, Rhoades's son, Caleb, joined him on the adventure. Eventually, Wakara's successor, Chief Tabby, denied access to the cave. Fulfilling their promise, Thomas and Caleb Rhoads never revealed the whereabouts of the mine, nor do we know for what church purpose the treasure retrieved from the mine was used. Over the years, the mine and its secret treasures have become somewhat of a fable in Utah lore.

But is the story about the lost Rhoades mine really a fable? Could the mine really exist? Several books have been written by talented scholars on the subject, including *Faded Footprints: The Lost Rhoades Mine and Other Hidden Treasures of the Uintas* by George A. Thompson and *The Gold of Carre-Shinob* by Kerry Ross Boren and Lisa Lee Boren. Also, historian and journalist Lynn Arave, writing for the *Deseret News* in the September 30, 2003 edition, gave additional insight into the idea that a treasure-filled cave might really exist somewhere in Utah's mountains—and not just one cave but many in several parts of the state. "There could be a lost mine for every major canyon in the Wasatch [Mountains]," he wrote. "For example, Taylor

Canyon, east of Ogden, supposedly has a lost gold mine, and bona fide abandoned mines are plentiful in Park City, Alta, Willard and other areas."

Who's to say if the mine will ever be found? No matter. Like all treasures, the fun is in the hunt and the imaginations of wealth if it were to be found.

OF FAITH AND A FORT

In 1800s Utah, travelers on the open desert would often come under attack by Indians. Weather was also sometimes harsh, and just the fatigue and hardship of the travel experience was enough to cause anxiety for many. One respite for those who came by central Utah was a fort named Cove that today is open for tours hosted by missionaries of the Church of Jesus Christ of Latter-day Saints.

"Built in 1867, Cove Fort was constructed as a safe stop for travelers, where they could find shelter, fresh water, and feed for livestock," reads an entry on the LDS website under "Historic Sites." "Go back in time to the days when travel was by horseback and covered wagon and discover what sort of accommodations a traveler could have expected."

The fort today, located about twenty-four miles north of Beaver in Millard County at a place called Cove Creek, is modeled as it would have appeared when it was in use more than one hundred years ago, and its friendly volunteer staff will greet visitors with smiles and answers to their questions. They take pride in the fort, an old-time marvel amid the backdrop of modern day; it is the only fort built by the church that still stands.

It started when Brigham Young called on Ira Hinckley to direct the construction of the 100.0-square-foot lava and limestone rock facility. For about seven months, between April and November 1867, workers quarried the rock from nearby and secured cedar and pine wood for the roof and doors at the east and west ends. The fort stands 18.5 feet tall and is about 4.0 feet thick at the footings and 2.5 feet thick at the top. The fort has twelve rooms, each furnished to look as it would have during its heyday. Its purpose is different today than what it was in the late 1800s. Information on Utah.com reads:

> *For more than twenty years Cove Fort served an important function, but as times changed so did the need for the fort. By 1890 the Church leased out the fort and after the turn of the century, sold it to the Otto Kesler family.*

Nearly one hundred years later, in 1988 the Hinckley family purchased the fort from the Keslers and made a gift of it to the Church as a historic site. Shortly afterward, efforts to restore the fort to its original condition were begun, and on May 21, 1994, Gordon B. Hinckley, later president of the Church of Jesus Christ of Latter-day Saints, dedicated the Historic Cove Fort Complex.

"It is our hope that Cove Fort will serve as a modern way station—not as a shelter from physical fatigue or protection from the elements," said Stephen D. Nadauld, speaking at the 1994 dedication, "rather, we hope it will serve as a spiritual way station where we can be reminded of the faith of our forefathers, where we can refresh our sense of sacrifice and obedience and our dedication to duty, where we can be reminded of the values of work, provident living, self-sufficiency, and family unity."

JACOB HAMBLIN'S GUN MISFIRES

There often was contention among the Mormons and Indians in Utah's early years, but there were periods and instances in which the two groups were friendly and got along with each other quite well. Jacob Hamblin, a member of the Quorum of the Twelve Apostles of the LDS Church during a volatile period in its history, was a friend to the Indians and was called the "Buckskin Apostle" because of the work he did among the tribes in Utah. The natives respected him, calling him simply "Jacob." At one time, however, they were angry with him and tracked him down to kill him, but his bravery turned their hearts. As one story goes, Hamblin one day had left Santa Clara to get supplies in Cedar City when two Indians came to his home and inquired of his whereabouts. After learning where he was headed, they tracked him down and told him of their intentions. Marlene Bateman Sullivan explained in an *Ensign* article from October 1984:

For a few moments there was silence. Then Jacob climbed down from the wagon seat, looked at the Indians, and pulled his shirt open—as if to say, "Shoot, I am unarmed."

The Indians stared a moment in silence. Then one muttered: "Can't Jacob, you've got my heart." They rode away.... Today he is considered the most influential and successful peacemaker and missionary among the Indian people in the territorial period.

Click-Click, No Bang

Jacob Hamblin was born on April 2, 1819, in Salem, Ohio, and joined the LDS Church one month before his twenty-third birthday in 1842. His first marriage ended when his wife, Lucinda, refused to go with him to Salt Lake City during the great migration. A devout follower of his Mormon faith, he believed that it was his duty to join the body of the Saints in the Rocky Mountains, his marriage notwithstanding. He packed his belongings, said a prayer and parted ways with his wife, bringing his four children with him. That was February 1849. That September, he met and married widow Rachel Judd in Council Bluffs, Iowa. Under the church's blessing, he married two other women and fathered children from each union. Once in Utah, he settled in Tooele in 1850. Soon after arriving, he and other brethren had a run-in with Indians. He drew his pistol to protect himself, as did his brethren, but each of their guns misfired. One gun not working properly could be an accident, but several?

"As I could not discharge my gun, I defended myself as well as I could with stones," he wrote. "I afterwards learned…that not one [of our company] was able to discharge his gun when within range of an Indian.…It appeared evident to me that a special providence had been over us…to prevent us from shedding the blood of the Indians. The Holy Spirit forcibly impressed me that it was not my calling to shed the blood of the scattered remnant of Israel, but to be a messenger of peace to them. It was also made manifest to me that if I would not thirst for their blood, I should never fall by their hands." God had intervened and, Hamblin believed, called him to be a "messenger of peace" to the native people.

Home Among the Indians

Four years after his arrival, President Brigham Young called Hamblin to serve as a missionary to the Paiute Indians in southern Utah. Hamblin, believing when a prophet called it was God's will, packed his belongings and led his family south, settling in a place called Santa Clara near St. George. After their first home was destroyed by flooding, Hamblin built a second home on a hill in 1863. It is this same home that, restored, stands today as a historical marker of the faith in southern Utah. An entry on Utah.com reads:

The Hamblin home, which is fronted by an immense green lawn, fallow wine orchards and a towering cottonwood, features a small formal mid-house entryway, flanked on either side by two bedrooms. Each bedroom features a small, steep, narrow stairwell which leads upstairs to a broad, impressive common area. Used for school-teaching, community meetings and family activities—Hamblin's community stature meant he was a father figure to many—this house-wide room has a vaulted ceiling, fireplace and a porch.

Eventually, Hamblin's daughters demanded privacy—they had been sharing the common area with the boys—and Hamblin added what tour guides today call the "girls' dormitory," an addition off the back of the house big enough for four beds and dressers.

Hamblin enjoyed the home only briefly, as he was called in 1869 to serve missions in Kanab, Utah, and parts of Arizona and New Mexico—each with a focus of administering to the Native Americans. His Santa Clara house today serves as a museum. Church missionaries give tours and instruct visitors on the history of the house and surrounding area. It's a cozy-looking house set amid a serene setting, with a garden and flowers on its property, making it look every bit as lived in as it did when Hamblin and his clan lived here in the mid-1800s.

Josie in the West

There's a small cabin in a place called Cub Creek in Dinosaur National Monument where time stands still. Not literally, of course, but figuratively. Perhaps just as lonely as it was in the early 1900s when Josie Bassett Morris built the cabin, the site located about thirty miles east of Vernal is now a tourist stop in Dinosaur National Monument. When you come here, perhaps with a self-guide flier in hand, you may find yourself feeling a little lonely for ole Ms. Morris. There isn't much around the site except the tall trees that give the property its shade, thick prairie grass that give the place an unkempt look, zigzagged wooden fences and kiosk signs that tell the story of the woman and her cabin. It's a cozy, and lonely, place to visit, not to mention work and live; Josie did just that for the better part of the last fifty years of her life. You can't help but wonder why. Not all of the grass here is tall, however, and if you walk into the pastureland and view the cabin from this perspective, you might find your answer. Viewing the homestead nestled in this niche of nature, you're likely to understand why Morris selected this spot as her solitude.

An Unconventional Woman

Getting to the site is half the fun, for along the way, you pass several places where the early Pueblo Indians carved or painted messages onto rocks long before even Josie arrived. She was just three years old when her family moved from Arkansas to the arid West in about 1877. The family settled in Brown's Park, Colorado, where they built a ranch where Josie grew and matured, perhaps developing more the traits of a ranch hand than the trimmings of a lady. It seemed to suit her well and prepared her for her future life in Cub Creek. She came here with her second husband, Ben Morris, in about 1913, but it wasn't until 1924 that she built the cabin, which has low-hanging windows and a dirt floor. It still stands in the quiet valley. She spent her next four decades here.

Morris didn't always live alone. Her son, Crawford McKnight (son of her first husband, Jim McKnight), and his family lived with her for several years. This gave her a chance to become acquainted with her grandchildren. They'd help her on the ranch, and she'd teach them how to milk a cow and feed a horse. She'd also play with them, as all good grandmothers do. When McKnight moved his family to Jensen, Utah, about ten miles away—a distance that seems much farther even with a modern vehicle because of the switchback dirt roads of the area—Josie was again left to work the ranch alone. She didn't mind. She was often visited by friends, including Butch Cassidy and outlaw members of his gang called the Wild Bunch.

More than once, Josie threw convention out the window—something you can do when you live by yourself in the rough of nature. For instance, tired of working in the long skirts that came with her from Brown's Park, she decided one day to start wearing pants, something most women didn't do in her day. But Josie wasn't like most women, and she also eventually cut her long red hair, wearing it short thereafter. By the time of her passing at age ninety in 1963, her red hair had turned white. Historian D. Robert Carter offered this glimpse of the unconventional woman:

> *Josie Bassett stands out as one of the most colorful characters in Uintah County's colorful past. She was a unique blend: a sweet, generous, loveable*

> *white-haired lady who occasionally rustled cattle, poached deer, and brewed bootleg whiskey to survive and help family and friends. For 50 years she lived alone in a cabin without plumbing, telephone, or electricity deep within what is now Dinosaur National Monument. Content among her flowers, gardens, orchards, cattle herds, and assorted domestic animals, she became a fascinating minor character in the pageant of the West.*

On the one hand, Josie was a serious-minded person who had little time for trivialities and hung out with known outlaws, but on the other hand, she was a remarkably caring woman who often went out of her way to help family members, friends and even odd acquaintances. Carter, who has done a fabulous job bringing her experiences to life in his own writings, explained that during one winter she lived in a dugout "so a homeless family could use her cabin":

> *After she sold most of her cattle to help her son, Josie would sometimes shoot deer out of season to provide meat for herself, her family, or needy neighbors. Necessity dictated this lawless action. Once a game warden stopped by shortly after she had killed a deer. When she invited him in for coffee and biscuits, as she did with most everyone, the warden said he was there to arrest her for poaching. Thinking he was serious, she confessed and took him to the freshly dressed carcass. Astounded, the warden said he had only been joking. Not knowing what to do with this sweet old lady, he let her off with a strong warning and then enjoyed her venison gravy over hot biscuits.*

Not many women—and probably not a lot of men—could do what Josie did: live alone in a cabin without electricity, running water or other household amenities in the secluded forest for the better portion of fifty years. Looking at it strictly as an endurance test, it was a remarkable—and likely remarkably lonely—feat to accomplish.

Before the Grim Reaper came knocking at her door, he spread a layer of ice one winter on which Josie slipped and broke her hip. Suffering from the injury for nearly a year, she eventually passed from this life on May 1, 1964, leaving her cozy cabin as one of Utah's historical gems.

HOW BUTCH CASSIDY GOT HIS NAME

His given name was Robert LeRoy Parker, but you know him as Butch Cassidy, one of the Old West's most infamous characters. The leader of the Wild Bunch had his roots in Utah.

Parker, the eldest of thirteen children, was born on April 13, 1866, in Beaver but grew up in Circleville. He likely was taught the teachings of the LDS faith as a young boy, as his parents and grandparents were members of the Mormon Church. His religious teachings seemed not to have stuck with him as he grew older. At age thirteen, he was arrested for breaking into a store and stealing a pair of coveralls. He left a note for the store owner, promising to return payment. But that wasn't good enough for the shopkeeper, and he called the authorities on the young man. As Parker grew older, he stepped further away from his religious upbringing by becoming a cattle rustler and horse thief. On June 24, 1889, he robbed his first bank—one of dozens of crimes he would commit in his unlawful career in the Old West. He didn't always work alone and eventually formed a gang of ten outlaws called the Wild Bunch, but the person he is most often associated with went by the name the Sundance Kid.

Fact or Fiction

There are so many stories about Parker that it's difficult to tell fact from fiction. That doesn't stop them from circulating, perhaps especially in southern Utah. "Sit down in a café in just about any town in Garfield, Piute or Iron county and ask about Butch Cassidy and it isn't hard to find someone who has a Butch Cassidy story," reads an article by Steven Law on KSL.com. "Cassidy stories drift about here like cotton from cottonwood trees. But verifying the truth of any of these stories is difficult to do this far after the fact. Anyone who knew Cassidy is long-since dead. Like the respectable outlaw that he was, he's still a hard man to track down. One starts to feel like they've entered the realm of Sasquatch, Elvis and the Loch Ness Monster. A Butch Cassidy story often starts like this, 'I heard this story from my dad/grandpa/grandma who heard it from his dad, who used to hang out with Butch Cassidy.'"

Even Parker's death is a mystery. Because he was pursued by bounty hunters and members of the Pinkerton clan, it is believed that Cassidy fled to South America in 1901, and using a different name, he and Sundance purchased property to operate a ranch. But their taste for the outlaw life eventually resurfaced, and their crime spree continued. The two ruffians then fled to Bolivia, where, by some accounts, he and Sundance died in a shootout with local lawmen in November 1908. Another account, however, claims that the daring duo returned to the United States, lived for many more years and passed away as old men.

Law seems to be right. When it comes to stories about Cassidy, "It's folk hero meets conspiracy theory meets six degrees of Kevin Bacon." In that light, it's difficult to say for sure how Parker received his more popular name, but here's one story that seems fairly plausible.

Call Me Butch

Not long after his first bank heist in Telluride, Colorado, Parker started using the name Cassidy. When he moved to Rock Springs, Wyoming, he started working a legitimate job at a butcher shop. Apparently, it inspired him to start using the name "Butch." And there you have it—Parker, Utah's infamous armed bandit, who grew up in a Mormon household but shunned his religious upbringing for a life of crime that started in his early teens, evolved into the infamous character that history has known for more than one hundred years as Butch Cassidy.

NEWSPAPER CONTROVERSY

An ambition of today's news organizations is to break the news before their competitors. Things weren't much different in the early days of American journalism, when reporters scoured their beats looking for the next big story. Reporters would rush back to the newsroom to write their stories or dictate them to an editor. Afterward, articles would be given to copy editors, who, often with visors on their heads to shield their eyes from the glare of the city room's bright lights, worked quickly to vet stories before they'd be worked into the print cycle. It was the ambition of every newspaper editor to get the news into print and onto the streets before their rivals, and to do that he needed ambitious reporters, savvy copy editors and skilled printer's devils.

Once an edition was printed, newsboys would take the papers to the street corners and shout the news of the day. The payoff would come when readers bought copies, when people in the know read the edition and when it sparked controversy, started a public discussion, made people think and sometimes changed public policy. Much has changed in recent years with modern newspapers, but it is the same dividend that makes the news business one worthy to be a part of today. The friendly feud to break news before a competitor is healthy for a free press, for the simple reason that it's not news if you've heard it before. It is what helps legitimize a news organization.

Something was different with Utah's two early newspapers. A rivalry existed between them, and it often wasn't friendly. Their feud stemmed not so much from breaking the same news first but rather from their individual biases and dislike for each other. One was the LDS-owned *Deseret News* and the other the secular *Salt Lake Tribune*. The first was a religious-leaning conservative paper and the second a liberal newspaper. They are still with us today, sharing a friendly competition, but their early editors would often attack each other in print and, at least once, according to the following story, on the street.

***

"I want you to get right down here on your knees and apologize for the lie you published about me last Sunday," said John Q. Cannon, the editor of the *Deseret News*.

"I never published any lie about you," replied Joseph Lippman, city editor of the rival newspaper, the *Salt Lake Tribune*.

"You did. Now I want you to apologize," Cannon demanded.

The controversy, as an article about Utah's newspaper wars by Hal Schindler explained in the April 14, 1996 issue of the *Salt Lake Tribune*, stemmed from an article Lippman had published about Cannon taking a young woman as a plural wife. Before becoming his bride, however, the woman was in league with a rival suitor. Cannon had, according to Lippman, arranged a mission call for the young man to get him out of the picture.

Now confronting Lippman on the corner of 100 South and State Street in downtown Salt Lake City, Cannon said it was all a lie and demanded that Lippman apologize.

"I will not," Lippman replied. That did it—Cannon lunged.

As Schindler wrote in his article:

> *Before the words were out of his mouth he found himself "flying through the air as if a cannonball had struck him." He was knocked about ten feet and landed on the back of his neck and shoulders. Before he could scramble to his feet, Cannon was on top of him with a "little rawhide" and was about to give him a taste of it, when the prostrate reporter "began to cry most piteously and beg for his life." Cannon gave him a couple of strokes across the head and hands and was about to apply some more, when police, alerted by Lippman's howls, arrived on the scene. Cannon pleaded guilty in court and was fined $15 for his "infraction of the law." He then hustled back to the* Deseret News *city room—to write the story for the next edition.*

The *Deseret News* and the *Salt Lake Tribune* were not Utah's only newspapers in the 1800s, nor were they the only ones at odds with each other. Their feuds are just better known. Many newspapers existed in Utah's earlier days. Papers such as the *Valley Tan* and *Keep-A-Pitchinin* are unfamiliar to most Utahns today, but they were names familiar to the territory's early residents. And there was the antagonistic paper called the *Daily Salt Lake Democrat*, which printed an article saying the editor of the *Salt Lake Daily Herald* "should be taken out on the desert and kicked to death by a band of wild asses."

"This invective was typical of the times," wrote Sherilyn Cox Bennion in an article on the Utah Education Network. She called the practice "American frontier journalism," explaining, "Although not all editors made name-calling their stock in trade, most had political preferences, and their opinions often embellished news reports as well as editorials."

Many of Utah's early papers have retired to the morgue, as has much of the controversy between Utah's two largest dailies. Modern newspapers, in Utah and elsewhere, face different challenges today. The dawn of the Internet in the 1990s brought fear into newsrooms across the country. Savvy news men and women saw the writing on the wall that one day their business would be challenged by articles published electronically. Now in the early twenty-first century, newspapers are still feeling the effects of the World Wide Web. Everything has gone mobile, and newspapers are losing their titles as "papers" as more and more go online. They are evolving into "news organizations." Many like the way in which news and information is produced, distributed and assimilated digitally—but not everyone. Some journalists long for the good ole days of newspapering, when the scent of musty papers was not an old or odd aroma at all but one that was welcomed every day, when ink-stained fingers were a casualty of another day in the newsroom and when the city desk bustled with harried reporters and cranky editors—even if their cranks showed up on the streets, as they did one day in the form of Lippman and Cannon.

The Circleville Massacre

A monument was erected on a day in early 2016 in the small Utah town of Circleville honoring some fifteen to twenty Paiute Indians who were killed by members of the Utah Militia in a little-known incident in 1866 called the Circleville Massacre. If you've never heard about the massacre, you're not alone. "It's an event that has been forgotten by many in the Paiute Tribe, by people in Circleville itself and, of course, by the general Utah population," Jedediah Rogers, a senior historian with the Utah Division of State History, told the *Salt Lake Tribune* for its April 22, 2016 edition—the day the monument was dedicated. The massacre was part of a larger conflict called the Black Hawk War.

The Black Hawk War

Mormon Prophet Joseph Smith spoke highly of the American Indians, referring to them as members of the Lost Tribes of Israel. Their day in the sun, so to speak, would come before Christ returns to the earth. They would, as the Book of Mormon teaches, "blossom as the rose." But in mid-1800s Utah, relationships with the native Indians were strained, and Mormons and Indians often found themselves on opposing sides. One conflict involved cattle.

"Burgeoning herds of hungry cattle drove their Mormon owners to usurp more and more grasslands, inadvertently playing primary roles in both the explosion of Mormon expansion into new areas and the cataclysmic loss of important traditional food resources for the Indians that resulted from it," reads a 2011 article by *Salt Lake Tribune* writer John A. Peterson. "Starving, weakened and more susceptible to indigenous and imported diseases, the Indians of Utah died off by the thousands during the early 1860s."

This and similar scenarios created conflict, sometimes escalating into bloody confrontations between the two groups in what has been called the Black Hawk War, named after an Indian chief. The seven-year "war," which started in 1865 and lasted until 1872, was not a continual clash of arms with frontline battles, as was the case in America's war between North and South, but it did involve many skirmishes, some of them deadly. The 2016 article continued:

> *The killings occurred at the height of Utah's Black Hawk War, which saw years of skirmishes between Mormon settlers and Utah's indigenous peoples.*
>
> *The Black Hawk War largely involved the Ute tribes in the northern parts of the state.*
>
> *But the tensions spread fear and suspicion throughout Utah's Mormon settlements.*
>
> *And like the more-famous Mountain Meadows Massacre, which saw the mass murder of a California-bound wagon train at the hands of Mormon settlers, Rogers said the Koosharem Band was inadvertently caught up in the middle of a devastating conflict.*
>
> *"The story is the victims," he said. "It's about a peaceful band of indigenous Utah Indians, the Paiute Tribe, being slaughtered by local Mormon settlers."*
>
> *While there has long been discussion among historians about the need to better recognize the Circleville Massacre, assistant LDS Church historian Richard Turley said the plans for a monument began taking shape over the past year.*
>
> *He said the massacre is unique because a significant loss of life was paired with a thorough evaporation from public awareness. Part of that is due, he said, to the population shifts in the area before and after the event.*

Monument as Reminder

In an April 19, 2016 story by Utah's Fox13 about the monument, Albert Winkler, a history archivist at Brigham Young University, told the station that the area's "white people panicked and thought the local Paiute Indians must have something to do with their enemies." They arrested a band of Indians, including women and children, and killed them after they tried to escape. "They took them out, hit them on the head, slit their throats in one of the greatest tragedies in Utah history," Winkler said. "After all these years, it's still gut wrenching."

Today, Circleville is a town in south-central Utah, in Piute County, about seventy-five miles northeast of Cedar City. The stone monument remembering the slain Native Americans adds ambience and reverence to this small town of some five hundred people. Adorned with a soaring eagle engraved above the inscription, it reads, "In remembrance of the innocent who were lost in this place so long ago. None of us can ever hope to describe the emotions that these people might have felt. All we can do is honor their existence as human beings."

The massacre is a dark episode in Utah history—and in the history of the Paiute Tribe—that shows what can happen when people's fears reach a point of frenzy: it clouds their vision, making them believe that even murder is justified if perceived injustices are righted. This kind of frenzied thinking has caused some of our own day's violent problems.

As disturbing as the incident is to even hear about, it can serve as a reminder to people living in the modern world, where, with its technology and busyness, race wars continue. "It is so easy to look upon a group of people negatively and repeat the same kinds of things," Winkler told the news station. "We have to draw the lines. The loss of human life is never excusable."

THE EXECUTION OF JOHN D. LEE

In 1857, a wagon company composed mostly of families from Arkansas was heading to California when it stopped in southern Utah to rest. It was a decision that cost many their lives. In a disturbing act of violence carried out by fanatical Mormons and several Paiute Indians, 120 men, women and children of the Baker and Fancher emigrant company were brutally slain. It was premeditated, coldblooded murder—one of the darkest episodes in Utah history. Many people, both Mormon and Paiute alike, committed the ghastly deed, but in the end, only one man paid the ultimate penalty for the unforgiveable sin. His name was John D. Lee.

The Massacre

It was a crisp, peaceful morning as the emigrants rose from their beds. They had camped in a quiet meadow not far from a babbling brook some thirty-five miles southwest of Cedar City. The tall grass swayed gently in the morning breeze as the aroma of rabbit and quail cooking over a campfire drifted among the morning throng. The serenity of the morning on this seventh day of September was shattered by the sound of a gunshot, followed by the cries of a mother as she saw her young child fall to the ground. The emigrants scarcely had time to collect their thoughts when more shots rang out, followed by the shrieks of Indians who were hiding in a nearby ravine. The crowd dispersed, running to their wagons and trying to find shelter. Within a few minutes, seven men from the emigrant company lay dead in the camp. It was but a foreshadowing of the horror that was to befall nearly the entire group.

For the next five days, the Baker-Fancher emigrant company huddled in the circle of their forty wagons, trying to protect themselves from the onslaught of the Indians—and militant Mormons who had dressed like Indians—that surrounded them. Things weren't looking good for the emigrants. Food and water were running low; some of the emigrants were sick. And then, on September 11, a white flag appeared, and members of the Utah Territorial Militia approached. Hope sprung in their hearts; the siege had come to an end, they thought.

They were deceived. It was these militia members, John D. Lee among them, who had enticed the local Indians to join them in the attack. Like the cowards they were, the militia members told the emigrants that to pacify the Indians, they must give up their arms and submit to the militia. No harm would come to them, they were told. The militia members would lead them safely out of harm's way, first to Pinto and then to Cedar City. Word quickly spread through camp, and the emigrants, not knowing what else to do under the circumstances, put their trust in this group of Mormons and surrendered their arms. The emigrants were told to separate into groups, the men into one group and the women and children in another. They marched the emigrant members several yards from camp so as to appear that they were taking them out of the hostile situation. Then, like devils incarnate, one of the militia members shouted the terrifying word, "Halt!" Without warning, the slaughter commenced.

The militia members had planned to kill everyone older than eight years, but during the frenzied slaughter, several young children also were murdered. One report says that an Indian stabbed an infant while its mother held the baby in her arms. The horrific episode, one of the darkest in Mormon and Utah history, lasted only five minutes, but when it was over, more than 120 men, women and children lay dead and bloodied on the prairie, their

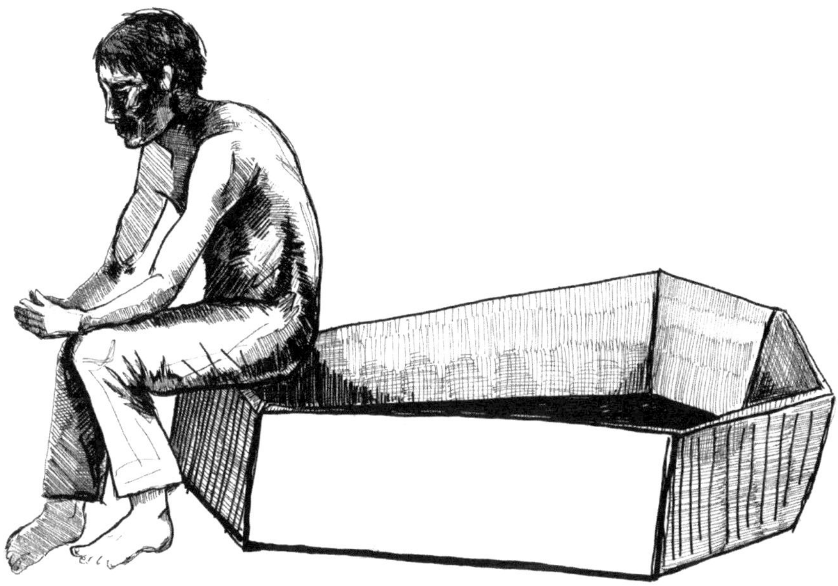

bodies shot, hacked, slashed or bludgeoned to death. Only 17 children were spared—the militia members deemed them too young to remember the ghastly deed. They were wrong. They had not understood the impact their savagery had on even the very young. Some eighty years after the massacre, one of the child survivors, Sarah Frances Baker, who was only three at the time of the massacre, recalled, "But even when you're that young, you don't forget the horror of having your father gasp for breath and grow limp, while you have your arms around his neck, screaming with terror….And you wouldn't forget it, either, if you saw your own mother topple over in the wagon beside you, with a big red splotch getting bigger and bigger on the front of her calico dress."

Who's to Blame?

The perpetrators never took responsibility for the massacre and instead blamed it on the Paiute Indians. But it was all orchestrated by this band of militia Mormons. Blame was often placed on Brigham Young and the LDS Church, especially in the early years after the massacre, because of the fanatical band of church members. Some had said that Young knew about the attack in advance and did nothing to prevent it; others said that he commanded it. If nothing else, others say, he helped spur the hatred for any gentile passing through Mormon territory because of his war rhetoric. In truth, Brigham Young did not order the attack, nor did he know about it until after it had occurred. He had caught wind of a siege going on but had sent a letter to John D. Lee telling him to let the emigrant company go and not harm the people. His letter arrived too late; the slaughter had already occurred.

Where the church faulted is not ever bringing any of the perpetrators to justice. In its earlier days, after the massacre, it also did not do much to honor those who had been slain. Instead, it tried to forget the dark day. It seemed to have done a good job. "The story of the most violent incident in the history of the America's overland trails remains among the West's most controversial historical subjects," wrote Will Bagley in his hallmark book *Blood of the Prophets*, "yet even students of the American West have nearly forgotten the event. Most Americans, including many Utahns, have never heard of it." It's understandable why the church doesn't like to talk much about this horrific episode, known to history as the Mountain Meadows Massacre. It knows that it's a dark spot, and talking about it does little to promote the goodwill of the church. All sane men and women recognize the crime for what it was. Former church president Joseph Fielding Smith called it a "bloody and diabolical deed" and the most "horrible and shocking crime ever perpetrated" in Utah.

On the 150th anniversary of the tragedy, September 11, 2007, the LDS Church, in an effort to honor the victims and acknowledge their posterity, held a ceremony dedicated to the victims and their families. Elder Henry B. Eyring, reading a prepared church statement at the event, said:

> *We express profound regret for the massacre carried out in this valley 150 years ago today and for the undue and untold suffering experienced by the victims then and by their relatives to the present time.*
>
> *A separate expression of regret is owed the Paiute people who have unjustly borne for too long the principal blame for what occurred during the massacre. Although the extent of their involvement is disputed, it is believed they would not have participated without the direction and stimulus provided by local church leaders and members.*

According to a *Deseret News* article by Carrie A. Moore published the next day:

> *Elder Eyring said that research by church historians…found that church President Brigham Young's message "conveying the will and intent…not to interfere with the immigrants arrived too late." The research also found that the "responsibility for the massacre lies with the local leaders of the Church of Jesus Christ of Latter-day Saints in the regions near Mountain Meadows who also held civic and military positions and with members of the church acting under their direction."*
>
> *Several hundred descendants of the victims traveled across the country to attend Tuesday's ceremony. Many of them had sought an apology from the church since the dedication eight years ago of a monument marking the burial site of some victims.*
>
> *Some have also petitioned the church to transfer to the federal government stewardship of the monument and surrounding lands the church has purchased to preserve the site that church President Gordon B. Hinckley has described as sacred ground.*
>
> *In addressing that proposal, Elder Eying said, "The church has worked with descendant groups…to maintain the monument and surrounding property and continues to improve and preserve these premises to make them attractive and accessible to all who visit. We are committed to do so in the future."*

The locale is a pretty spot in rural southern Utah, where the wind still rustles the prairie grass. It's easy to feel reverent here, if not a bit haunted, as you consider the lives that were lost in this fertile valley. Several monuments decorate the area, including a marker that lists the victims' names. The largest of the monuments is a stone pillar that honors those who came here to rest for a few days and instead found eternal sleep in its meadow.

The Guilty Scapegoat

John D. Lee has been called a scapegoat because out of the many men involved in the massacre, only he was tried, prosecuted and punished for the crime. It also has been debated just how much Lee was involved in the massacre. It's said that he bragged about his part in the incident for the first few weeks but then spent the next twenty years denying that he had anything to do with it. But his own confession, printed here, which he gave before his death in 1877, seems to qualify his involvement in the heinous crime. An article about Lee on the PBS website reads:

> *Lee's involvement in the massacre—the extent of which is still vigorously disputed and will probably never be known—was to haunt him for the next two decades, and would ultimately lead to his execution. He had written a letter to Brigham Young shortly after the massacre which laid the blame squarely on the Paiute Indians, but even among his own neighbors rumors of Lee's guilt abounded. In 1858 a federal judge came to southwestern Utah to investigate the massacre and Lee's part in it, but Lee went into hiding and local Mormons refused to cooperate with the investigation. Folk songs dating back to this year blamed Lee for the massacre. A warrant for his arrest remained outstanding.*
>
> *Although the church sought to lower Lee's profile, by removing him as a probate judge, the Mormon leadership continued to return his immense loyalty. In 1860, Brigham Young visited one of Lee's mansions and publicly praised his personal industriousness and communal economic contributions. In 1861 the residents of Harmony, Utah, elected him as their presiding elder.*
>
> *But Lee could not escape the legacy of Mountain Meadows. By the late 1860s, his diary, and letters from several of his wives, speak of persistent harassment by his Mormon neighbors for his connection with the massacre, including threatening letters and the ostracization of his children. In 1870 a Utah paper openly condemned Brigham Young for covering up the massacre. That same year Young exiled Lee to a remote part of northern Arizona and excommunicated him from the church, instructing his former confidant to "make yourself scarce and keep out of the way."*

The Confession of John Doyle Lee

As a duty to myself, my family, and mankind at large, I propose to give a full and true statement of all that I know and all that I did in that unfortunate affair, which has cursed my existence, and made me a wanderer from place to place for the last nineteen years, and which is known to the world as the Mountain Meadows Massacre.

I have no vindictive feeling against any one; no enemies to punish by this statement; and no friends to shield by keeping back, or longer keeping secret, any of the facts connected with the Massacre.

I believe that I must tell all that I do know, and tell everything just as the same transpired. I shall tell the truth and permit the public to judge who is most to blame for the crime that I am accused of committing. I did not act alone; I had many to assist me at the Mountain Meadows. I believe that most of those who were connected with the Massacre, and took part in the lamentable transaction that has blackened the character of all who were aiders or abettors in the same, were acting under the impression that they were performing a religious duty. I know all were acting under the orders and by the command of their Church leaders; and I firmly believe that the most of those who took part in the proceedings, considered it a religious duty to unquestioningly obey the orders which they had received. That they acted from a sense of duty to the Mormon Church, I never doubted. Believing that those with me acted from a sense of religious duty on that occasion, I have faithfully kept the secret of their guilt, and remained silent and true to the oath of secrecy which we took on the bloody field, for many long and bitter years. I have never betrayed those who acted with me and participated in the crime for which I am convicted, and for which I am to suffer death.

My attorneys, especially Wells Spicer and Wm. W. Bishop, have long tried, but tried in vain, to induce me to tell all I knew of the massacre and the causes which led to it. I have heretofore refused to tell the tale. Until the last few days I had intended to die, if die I must, without giving one word to the public concerning those who joined willingly, or unwillingly, in the work of destruction at Mountain Meadows.

To hesitate longer, or to die in silence, would be unjust and cowardly. I will not keep the secret any longer as my own, but will tell all I know.

At the earnest request of a few remaining friends, and by the advice of Mr. Bishop, my counsel, who has defended me thus far with all his ability, notwithstanding my want of money with which to pay even his expenses while attending to my case, I have concluded to write facts as I know them to exist.

I cannot go before the Judge of the quick and the dead with out first revealing all that I know, as to what was done, who ordered me to do what I did do, and the motives that led to the commission of that unnatural and bloody deed.

The immediate orders for the killing of the emigrants came from those in authority at Cedar City. At the time of the massacre, I and those with me, acted by virtue of positive orders from Isaac C. Haight and his associates at Cedar City. Before I started on my mission to the Mountain Meadows, I was told by Isaac C. Haight that his orders to me were the result of full

> *consultatation* [sic] *with Colonel William H. Dame and all in authority. It is a new thing to me, if the massacre was not decided on by the head men of the Church, and it is a new thing for Mormons to condemn those who committed the deed.*

Only God, who is the judge of all men, knows the truth of the matter. And as the scriptures read, vengeance is his. What we do know is that 120 men, women and children lost their lives in a senseless and bloody act of violence. Because of the sheer number of those slain, we also know that it was more than one person who committed the atrocity. Lee, however, became the scapegoat for all of the perpetrators. He was executed in 1877, nearly twenty years after the massacre, in the very meadow where the terrible events of September 1857 took place. The manner of execution was by firing squad. Lee sat on a coffin at the edge of a grave, and when the bullet struck him, his body fell into the coffin. Before his death, however, Mormon history's most infamous character hauntingly remarked, "I have but little to say this morning. Of course I feel that I am at the brink of eternity, and the solemnities of eternity should rest upon my mind at the present….I am ready to die. I trust in God. I have no fear. Death has no terror."

Part V
Progressive People

Like people, states grow and mature and come into their own identity. Utah developed its identity early on, but the ensuing decades saw changes and an evolution of sorts within some of its long-standing traditions. The people who make up the state, past and present, are skilled, talented, entrepreneurial types who will continue to shape the state into the unforeseeable future. Utah residents are progressive. It doesn't matter if they're LDS or Catholic, white or black, religious or secular, an entrepreneur or a blue-collar worker, a born-and-bred Utahn or an emigrant—for the most part, Utahns possess forethought and vision and are not afraid to work hard to make a difference. A lot of people throughout its history have worked extremely hard to make the state what it is today. And Utahns are still sharing their vision, talents and skills. Here are a few tales of progressive moments in Beehive State history.

Colored by Diversity

Although it shouldn't always be the case, in some circumstances men have to prove themselves to their peers before they are generally accepted among the group. That's how it was for a group of black soldiers that came through Utah soon after it attained statehood. It wasn't until two years later, after the men had served their country in battle, that the returning soldiers were welcomed.

"When an all-black infantry unit came to Utah in 1896, state leaders sent a formal complaint to the War Department, insisting the soldiers were not welcome," Paul Rolly, a writer for the *Salt Lake Tribune*, explained in a June 9, 2016 article. "Two years later, after the 24th Infantry battalion returned from fighting in the Spanish-American War in Cuba, a parade in downtown Salt Lake City saluted the soldiers. It remained a time of racial divides and deep prejudices, but familiarity with the soldiers led to their acceptance."

It may not seem all that ironic that state lawmakers at first had such a difficult time with the black infantry. Such was the political and racial climate of the time. But in another respect, it is quite absurd that the black infantry was not better welcomed. Black men and women, both Mormon and non-Mormon, who came to Utah before and after it attained statehood, played important roles in the settlement and development of the territory.

The state's black population has grown slowly but steadily over the decades. According to the most recent census statistics, black residents comprise only 1.8 percent of Utah's more than 2 million residents. Some of the first black men who came to the area were James P. Beckworth and Jacob Dodson, members of exploratory and fur trapping expeditions that visited the territory some twenty-five years before the pioneers arrived. We don't hear about them often, but when the Latter-day Saints arrived in the Great Basin, among the throng were black men and women and their families, including Green Flake, Oscar Crosby and Hark Lay. Some of them were baptized members of the LDS Church, and others were not. Most were slaves who had come with the pioneers to settle in the Mountain West and worked on farms.

Isaac James and his wife, Jane, were the first free blacks to settle in Utah, which they did in the fall of 1847. Having married in Nauvoo, Illinois, before the Saints' forced evacuation from that state, where they had built a temple, the couple, along with their two sons, Sylvester and Silas, made the journey west to regroup with the members of their faith. Other black men and their families who arrived early in Utah included Elijah Abel and Frederic Sion, also of the LDS faith. They as well as other minority groups, such as the growing Hispanic and Asian populations that later came to work on the railroad, helped settle and build the territory.

By the 1890s, the black community started building churches in the area, giving more diversity to the area's religious climate. Reverend James Saunders, for instance, appointed an association to build an African Methodist Episcopal Church. LDS Church president Wilford Woodruff even pledged support in the sum of fifty dollars to the cause. Later, the Baptist Prayer

Band—which started meeting in the home of Emma Jackson for prayers and Bible study, according to an article by Miriam Murphy as found on Utah History to Go—evolved into Salt Lake City's Calvary Baptist Church. One of this church's fundraising events was a 'possum dinner, complete with "yams, hoe cake, tomatoes, corn, hot biscuits coffee, ice cream, and cake," Murphy wrote, and it attracted the all-black community as well as some visitors. The effort seemed to have worked. Reverend J.W. Washington and his congregation on June 29, 1902, "welcomed visitors at a reception in the new chapel at 472 East Second South."

Black residents in Utah and other minority groups continued to contribute to the state's diversity and well-being, but that doesn't mean that everything was bliss. As in other places across the country, black residents in Utah faced racial prejudice. It didn't help that the LDS Church, while never segregating congregations, had from about 1852 prohibited blacks from attaining the full blessings of church membership by not allowing ordination of black men to the priesthood. That all changed more than 120 years later, on a warm day in the summer of 1978.

DECLARING A NEW ERA

The Lord "doeth that which is good among the children of men," reads a passage from the Book of Mormon, "and he doeth nothing save it be plain unto the children of men; and he inviteth them all to come unto him and partake of his goodness; and he denieth none that come unto him, black and white, bond and free, male and female; and he remembereth the heathen; and all are alike unto God, both Jew and Gentile" (Second Book of Nephi 26:33). These verses echo what the Apostle Peter taught in the Bible: "Of a truth I perceive that God is no respecter of persons: But in every nation he that feareth him, and worketh righteousness, is accepted of him" (Acts 10:34–35).

And yet, since at least 1852, black male members of the LDS Church could not hold the priesthood. That changed on a warm day in June 1978 when church president Spencer W. Kimball and the Quorum of the Twelve Apostles issued a declaration positioning the church's stance on blacks and their relationship to membership and the priesthood. It was a momentous day in LDS Church history, one that will continue to bless the lives of black Mormons for generations to come.

Elder Bruce R. McConkie, one of the apostles with President Kimball when the decision was discussed in the Salt Lake Temple, recounted the experience. While the church's statement on black members and the priesthood was issued as a "Declaration," Elder McConkie called the new policy a "revelation." "I was present when the Lord revealed to President Spencer W. Kimball that the time had come, in His eternal providences, to offer the fullness of the gospel and the blessings of the holy priesthood to all men," Elder McConkie wrote. "I was present, with my brethren of the Twelve and the counselors in the First Presidency, when all of us heard the same voice and heard the same message from on high."

The brethren had gathered in the temple for discussion and prayer about the role of black men and women in the Church, a topic that had for some time weighed on the mind of President Kimball. During the prayer, President Kimball asked that the Lord forgive and purify the brethren so they could be more in tune with his will. "He counseled freely and fully with the Lord," McConkie explained, "was given utterance by the power of the Spirit, and what he said was inspired from on high."

After the initial prayer, President Kimball asked the brethren if any would like to "express their feelings and views as to the matter in hand," which the brethren did "freely and fluently and at considerable length." Afterward, it was suggested the brethren again unite in formal prayer, with the prophet acting as voice:

> *It was during that prayer that the revelation came. The Spirit of the Lord rested mightily upon us all; we felt something akin to what happened on the day of Pentecost and at the dedication of the Kirtland Temple. From the midst of eternity, the voice of God, conveyed by the power of the Spirit, spoke to his prophet. The message was that the time had now come to offer the fulness of the everlasting gospel, including celestial marriage, and the priesthood, and the blessings of the temple, to all men, without reference to race or color, solely on the basis of personal worthiness. And we all heard the same voice, received the same message, and became personal witnesses that the word received was the mind and will and voice of the Lord....All doubt and uncertainty fled.*

There have been many thoughts expressed and many personal philosophies implied as to why the church had previously denied black men the priesthood—something that seems to have started with the administration of Brigham Young in about 1852. An essay by the LDS

Church titled "Race and the Priesthood" and published on its website generically explains that it was "an era of great racial division in the United States. At the time, many people of African descent lived in slavery, and racial distinctions and prejudice were not just common but customary among white Americans. Those realities, though unfamiliar and disturbing today, influenced all aspects of people's lives, including their religion." No matter the reasoning at the time for the racial ban, what matters today is that the church now offers the fullness of church membership to all men and women, no matter their race or color. The only qualification is individual worthiness as measured by certain standards such as, among others, moral cleanliness, honesty and faith in the Lord Jesus Christ. This supports the notion that God judges not by outward appearance but by what is imprinted on the heart.

Failed Dreams of a Mining Engineer

It happened to a lot of gold-hungry men in the 1800s—they'd hear of an opportunity to become wealthy, and through ambition, perseverance and hard work, they'd find a nugget, perhaps not of gold but of truth: luck was not in their favor. They wound up just as poor as when they started their mining adventure. Such was the case with lowly Edwin Thatcher Wolverton, a mining engineer from Maine who came to Utah with gold-plated dreams.

Wolverton, like many in his time, had heard stories about Spanish mines hidden in Utah's mountains. He obtained a mining claim and started his search in the Henry Mountains in the southeast portion of Utah. What riches awaited him, he may have thought. But there was one thing more: he'd need a mill to process all of that ore he just knew he'd retrieve from this pocket of Mother Earth. He built it in about 1921 on Mount Pennell.

Mother was being obstinate, however, and tried Wolverton's patience. For years, the mining engineer worked his skill in the mountains, filing mining claim after mining claim, but in all that time, he retrieved nary a wit of gold. Year after year it was the same—after expending valuable time and resources in his search for riches, he came up empty handed. Wolverton, either coming to his senses or just being too tired to continue, finally gave up his search for the Spanish mines and closed his mill in 1929. His once gold-plated dreams were now covered with dust. And it wasn't even gold dust.

Wolverton's Success

Actually, Wolverton had been sitting on his gold mine all along. Although he never found the alleged Spanish mines of the Henry Mountains, in the process of searching for them he had built an ingenious mill that, in recent years, has become a historic preservation project of the Bureau of Land Management. The mill included "a large table saw in one end," reads information from the BLM.

> *With this, he could cut lumber for his needs as well as those of many of his remotely located neighbors, thereby obtaining supplies and bartered services. This feature made the Wolverton Mill unique because it combined both wood cutting and ore crushing operations under one roof. Besides being unique in function, the Wolverton Mill was also unique in construction. Most log structures of the time made use of some form of log notching and overlapping to tie the walls together. Wolverton cut his logs off evenly, stacked them, and used steel spikes inserted vertically through the ends of the logs to build the mill walls. The walls were built in sections and braced with heavy posts. There were no other mills in the Southwest like this one.*

There was a little gold that did run through the mill, but not for long. Despite its lack of use in Wolverton's day, the mine serves a "unique monument to mining, perseverance, and genius," according to the BLM. Wolverton died at the age of sixty-seven in 1929, but his mill continues to stand as an emblem of his determination, patience and perseverance. The agency moved the mill in 1974 to its present location in Hanksville at the BLM Henry Mountain Field Station. Restoration work was done in 1988.

ROBERT NEWTON BASKIN GETS A HEADSTONE

He may not have been a hero to the early Latter-day Saints, but that's no reason he shouldn't be recognized with a proper grave marker. Robert Newton Baskin, a prominent citizen in early Utah history who later fell into obscurity, wasn't recognized with a proper memorial until July 2014. He died in 1918. The reason his burial site was long without a headstone may have something to do with how he was viewed by leaders of the state's dominant religion.

Why the Hate?

Baskin was a champion of the law, but he was not a fan of Mormonism—nor were LDS leaders fond of him. Perhaps this is the reason his name is little mentioned in Utah history. In an article published on May 23, 2014, in the *Salt Lake Tribune*, historian Eileen Hallet Stone explained the animosity that some church leaders had toward the man. "Baskin was measured among the most hated Gentiles of Utah," she wrote. "Apostle George Q. Cannon thought him 'a cruel and unrelenting enemy.' Joseph F. Smith prayed he would be 'made blind, deaf and dumb unless he would repent his wickedness.' LDS historian Orson Ferguson Whitney described him as the 'human mainspring of nearly every anti-Mormon movement that Utah has known.'"

These harsh statements seem even more vehement coming from brethren of a church that teaches love, respect and forgiveness. The reason the leading brethren of the early church did not like him was because he used his efforts to thwart several aspects of the Mormon cause. Non-Mormons, however, championed his causes, especially the legislation he drafted that helped put an end to polygamy in Utah.

Baskin was born on December 20, 1837, in Hillsboro, Ohio, and studied law with the James H. Thompson firm in Salem, Ohio, before moving to Utah to practice his profession. Baskin was ambitious and enterprising, and Utah and its quirky Mormons seemed to offer him plenty of opportunities and challenges. Fighting polygamy was a big deal to him, but so was convicting John D. Lee for his involvement in the bloody episode of 1857 known to history as the Mountain Meadows Massacre. Lee was the only person convicted for the crime, although there were many culprits who had killed the more than 120 men, women and children on that fall day in southern Utah. Baskin sought justice for the crime, and if nothing else, he helped send at least one of the perpetrators to the grave. Lee was executed by firing squad in 1877.

Baskin was tenacious, a trait useful in sustaining and defending the law but one that some early Utahns didn't seem to like. Of interesting note, Baskin became friends to a Dr. Robinson, who once had plans to build a public hospital, Utah's first, something you'd think any community would be proud to adopt. Not so, Salt Lake City. Police tore it down and told Robinson that he'd have to go elsewhere for such a venture, an action that, according to the stories, seemed to have drawn little sympathy from Brigham Young. A *New York Post* article dated November 7, 1867, published an alleged quote from the church president in which he said, "The band of men had done wrong; that instead of going by night to destroy the building, they should have gone through it in broad day."

Such was the volatile era for men like Baskin in 1800s Utah, where Mormons often still viewed non-LDS newcomers to the territory as unwanted gentiles. The Latter-day Saints were, in many ways, still trying to get a foothold in their new home, but they kept confronting obstacles from outsiders like Baskin and Robinson. The two men had become good friends, but this only caused another trial for Baskin. His friend Robinson was assassinated on October 22, 1866.

Finally, a Headstone

Baskin died at the age of eighty on August 25, 1918. His body was laid to rest in an unmarked grave at the Mount Olivet Cemetery in Salt Lake City. It wasn't until July 30, 2014, that Baskin's grave was given a proper headstone. It's a simple marker engraved with the family name, a U.S. flag and a Masonic symbol. On the right is his wife's name, Olive L. Gardner (1840–1890), and to the left is his, Robert Newton (1837–1918). Below these is the name of a daughter, Katherine C. Baskin Peyton (1869–1888), and at the bottom is written, "Infant Girl Unknown." Records indicate that this second child was Della Baskin, who may have been six or seven years old when she died, years distant from being an infant.

A TALE OF THE CAPITOL THEATRE

Walk downtown Salt Lake City and you'll see the past and present displayed in its buildings—architecture from yesteryear as well as more modern times. As an example, the Salt Lake Temple, which took forty years to build and was dedicated in 1893, is a Gothic-spired building that has become an iconic symbol of the LDS faith. Across the street to the north of the temple is the massive Conference Center, which embodies everything that is stately modern. Instead of these two architectural masterpieces clashing, they complement each other and the city. That's how it is downtown—one building represents a now bygone era and another our more modern day.

Built in 1913, the Capitol Theatre was known originally as the Orpheum Theater, one of many in a chain of Orpheum Theaters built across the country in the early twentieth century. The Italian Renaissance–style theater cost $250,000 to build and was designed by G. Albert Lansburgh, who included "lighting, ventilation and water sprays in case of fire, all of which were state-of-the-art technology for their day," according to an August 23, 2014 *Deseret News* article published in honor of the building's 101st birthday:

> *"In point of architecture, appointments, size and all the latest improvements, Salt Lake can now truthfully boast of having one of the finest theaters in America," stated a* Deseret Evening News *article published to announce the theater's opening.*
>
> *The vaudeville house first opened its doors on Saturday, Aug. 2, 1913, and received a positive response.*
>
> *In a review following the inaugural performance, the* Deseret News *wrote that the Orpheum Theater opened with "a blaze of brilliance" and that "long before 8 o'clock, the street in front of the lobby was congested by the arrival of throngs of automobiles."*

The theater's first shows were vaudeville performances, but it expanded its offerings in 1923 when it started showing silent films. As such, period stars such as Charlie Chaplin, Douglas Fairbanks, Lillian Gish, Rudolph Valentino, Buster Keaton and others would have graced the screen. Music to complement the films came from live piano playing set up inside the theater. Things changed in 1929, when the first talkies were shown, but by this time, the theater was operating under a different name, having been sold two years before. The name stuck, even after a renovation in 1978, and it is still known as the Capitol Theatre.

Not all of its history has been pleasant, however. The building caught fire on July 4, 1949, during a matinee performance in the theater, leading to its evacuation. Firefighters were able to put out the blaze, according to the *Deseret News*, but not before the flames claimed the life of one of its ushers, a seventeen-year-old boy named Richard L. Duffin.

Perhaps because of the tragedy, some urban legends started about the building being haunted. Witnesses to alleged paranormal events said they've heard loud noises and doors slamming in the building when no one else was around. Shadowy figures also have been reported in the building, and at least one man told the *Salt Lake Tribune* in an August 21, 2012 article that he was attacked by an unseen entity. For the most part, however, the theater has been a place of fun-filled entertainment for the thousands who've come here to sit under its domed roof and watch art come alive on the screen and on the stage. Popular acts such as Tchaikovsky's *The Nutcracker*, Andrew Lloyd Webber's musical *Cats* and the same composer's retelling of *The Phantom of the Opera* all have been performed in the theater. In its earlier days, perhaps the silent movie *The Phantom of the Opera* had been shown here, making it one of few theaters in the country that displayed a movie and musical/play by the same title on the stage.

There's no doubt that times have changed. The vaudeville acts that were popular in the 1920s and '30s have been replaced by more contemporary classics, and silent pictures have all but gone the way of the dodo. But truly stately buildings such as Utah's Capitol Theatre keep something of their past alive in their architecture and elegance. This Salt Lake City building is a high-brow example of both. The building today serves as the home base for Ballet West, Children's Dance Theater and Utah Opera. It remains one of the state's most popular and beloved buildings.

UFC?

When Colonel Harland Sanders created his famous fried chicken recipe, he started selling the food in a roadside diner in his home state of Kentucky during the Great Depression. It wasn't until years later that he had the idea of turning his business into a franchise, which he called Kentucky Fried Chicken (better known today as KFC). But it isn't the Bluegrass State that lays claim to opening Sanders's first franchised restaurant. That recognition goes to Utah.

Utah got its first taste of Sanders's chicken in 1952 at Harman Café, located at 3900 South and State Street. Colonel Sanders, on his way to Australia, stopped in Salt Lake City to meet with owner Pete Harman. He wanted Harman to try his chicken recipe. Opting to go into his kitchen instead of taking a tour of the valley, the colonel prepared his original recipe. Pete; his wife, Arlin; and his nephew, Bob, were all soon licking their fingers.

Duty called, and according to a January 12, 2012 *Deseret News* article by Lee Benson, Sanders left the next morning for Australia, while Harman went to his café and put the colonel's chicken on his menu. Because Sanders was from Kentucky and it was fried chicken, they simply named it "Kentucky Fried Chicken." The rest, as they say, is history.

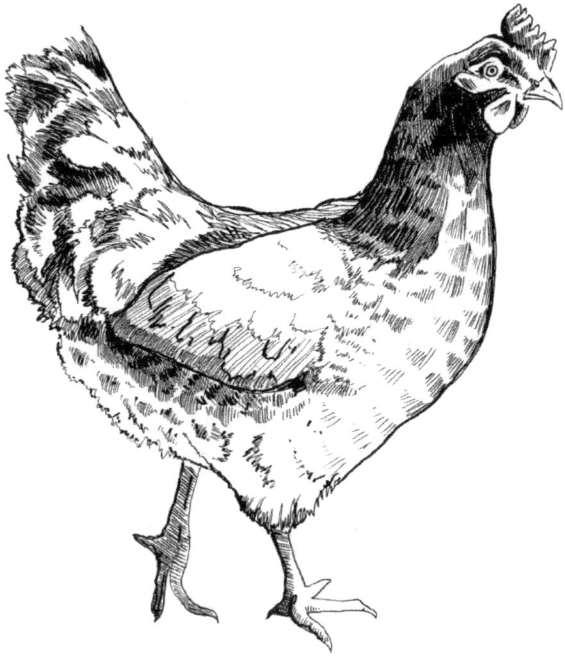

The popularity of the chicken that was "finger lickin' good" prompted Sanders to start franchising his chicken formally, and restaurants started popping up across the country, giving the traditional hamburger and fries fast-food chains a run for their money and consumers another menu option. By 1964, Sanders was feeling overwhelmed and sold his business, but its original recipe has remained the same.

Since the first Kentucky Fried Chicken store opened in Utah, maybe it should be called UFC.

Part VI
Taller Tales

Utah has a history of cowboys, Indians and Mormons, spiritual highs and lows and figures who paint the history with color. And then there are the monsters. Every state has them, of course—legends and folklore that also help paint their history. Utah's alleged monsters come in the form of mysterious water creatures, but there's also the red-eyed wolves and, of course, stories about that popular creature that likes to haunt Utah's forests and, sometimes, its neighborhoods—you know him as Bigfoot. Here you'll read about some of Utah's legends and pieces of folklore, including a creepy fellow who in his day allegedly liked to rob graves.

Monsters

Underneath the green waters of Utah Lake swim a variety of fish species—catfish, crappie, white bass and others. But if you were to have lived in Utah in the 1860s, you might very well have believed that a sea serpent of sorts swam with the fish. Utah Lake is one of several waters in the region with stories of water monsters that, every once in a while, would break the surface to show unwary bystanders the terror that lies in the murky deep.

According to an article by Lynn Arave in the September 23, 2001 edition of the *Deseret News*, gleaning information from Utah historian D. Robert Carter, a man named Henry Walker claimed that in 1864 he had seen the monster that haunts Utah Lake break the surface and stay above water long enough for him to describe, at least partially, what it looked like. It resembled "a large snake," he said, "with the head of a greyhound." Two other men in the 1860s reported seeing a similar creature, describing it as having "wicked-looking black eyes."

While some claimed to believe the stories, others said that Utah Valley residents made up the tales. Utah Lake wasn't the only body of water in which alleged monsters were seen. A newspaper called the *Daily Corrine* in Box Elder County published an article noting that stories of the Utah Lake monster were a hoax, "claiming that the monster actually lived at the north end of the Great Salt Lake, as evidence by recent sightings there." Go figure.

The Creature at Bear Lake

Stories about the Bear Lake Monster were told to the pioneers when they began to settle Cache Valley in northern Utah in the 1860s and became popular after newspaperman Joseph C. Rich wrote an article for the *Deseret News*. The article, "Monsters in Bear Lake," appeared in the July 31, 1868 edition. Rich shared the Indian legend but included additional witnesses of the alleged monster. Not long after the article was published, others came forward to share their encounters with the giant of the deep, a mysterious creature that became known as the Bear Lake Monster.

A man named C.M. Johnson, according to the book *Folklore in the Bear Lake Valley*, claimed that he saw the head and long neck of a creature rise from the water's surface. Even Brigham Young seemed to have believed the stories,

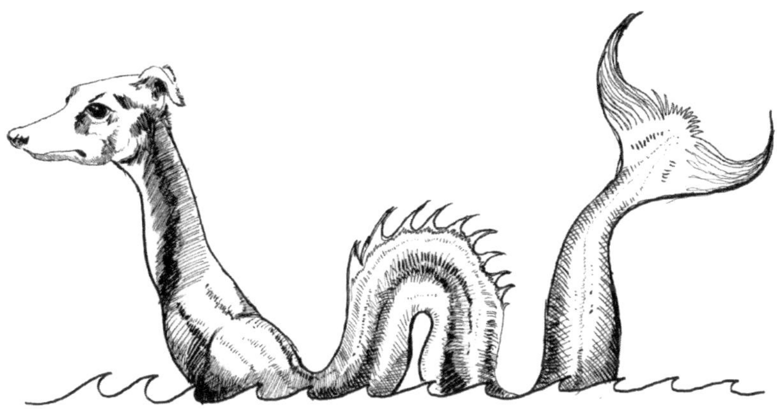

for he supposedly offered rope to a hunting expedition to snare the monster. According to another story, there wasn't just one monster but a whole family of them. In 1871, the *Salt Lake City Herald* reported that a man had captured a young member of the monster family near Fish Haven. "This latter-day wonder is said to be about twenty feet in length, with a mouth sufficiently large to swallow a man without any difficulty, and is propelled through the water by the action of its tail and legs."

Interestingly, twenty years after Rich's article was published, he confessed that he had made up the tales after he heard the Indian stories, hoping to attract attention to the area. Rich's confession didn't stop the stories from circulating, however, and more eyewitnesses reported seeing the strange water creature. Descriptions have varied—the monster may resemble a walrus, a large carp, a dragon, a crocodile or a duck-billed creature and range in size anywhere from twenty feet to ninety feet long; it's also able to reach swimming speeds of up to sixty miles per hour!

The Moon Lake Monster

Tales about a large water serpent that inhabits Moon Lake, a scenic lake in the rough wilds of northeastern Utah's Duchesne County, started when it was discovered long ago that parts of the lake have no known bottom. Some people believe that the lake has subterranean passages that go beneath the mountains to the Cache National Forest lake system. Christina Bailey, a cultural anthropologist with the Ashley National Forest, told me so when I interviewed her for a story about the legend in my book *Haunted Utah*. Studies have been conducted, she said, and parts of the lake are reported to have no bottom. Bailey said that she's never seen such a monster but that it's common knowledge in the area that such a creature might really exist.

In an unknown article printed in my grandmother's self-published life history, the author describes once seeing a strange "V" formation in the waters of Moon Lake as something moved toward shore. The writer thought it was a school of fish, or perhaps a beaver, but quickly found out it was neither. Could it have been the Moon Lake Monster?

> *I focused the binoculars again on the apex of the V as it approached the near shore. The binoculars gave me clear enough* [sight] *to know this was no beaver. And I don't know of any fish species that schools in a goose-like V formation like that, either....* [A]*nd it was the only thing moving on the*

lake. It zigged toward the far shore, not sharply, but rather at a wider-than-right angle from the direction it traveled as it neared me. As it headed away, I observed the apex from the back and could see nothing breaking the surface; only the rounded push of water at one point, seeming just below the surface. The point looked the same, coming and going. After another couple of approaches and retreats toward and away from the shore, the ripple gradually disappeared downstream in the sun's brightening reflection on the lake.

Where Have All the Monsters Gone?

In our day of satellites and digital photography, you'd think that if lake monsters truly existed they'd have been captured by someone with a smartphone. But sightings of Utah's alleged monsters have been few and far between, although the legends still persist. Even if it's never been confirmed that unknown creatures swim in the waters of several Utah lakes, it is fun to think that, just maybe, a giant lurks beneath the waves. Mother Nature sometimes keeps her secrets hidden well. As for the tales, historian and journalist Lynn Arave explained that lake monsters were "fashionable" in the 1870s but eventually fell "out of favor....There was one sighting and a brief upsurge in 1921 for the Utah Lake monster," the *Deseret News* article reads, "but then it 'sank in the depths of the lake' and apparently hasn't been seen since."

THE HEART OF TIMPANOGOS

When two people are in love, the world seems a much brighter place. Young Ucanogos, an Indian maiden, knew this—her love for the brave Timpanac, and his love for her, brought warmth to her heart and a smile to her face. She imagined that one day the two would be united as husband and wife in the tradition of their tribes. There was only one problem with this wish: Ucanogos and Timpanac came from different Indian tribes, and it wasn't customary for them to intermarry. But maybe her father, who was an Indian chief, and with the blessing of the Great Spirit, could allow this one encroachment to tradition. But there was another problem: Timpanac wasn't the only one who noticed the pretty Ucanogos. How could she prove

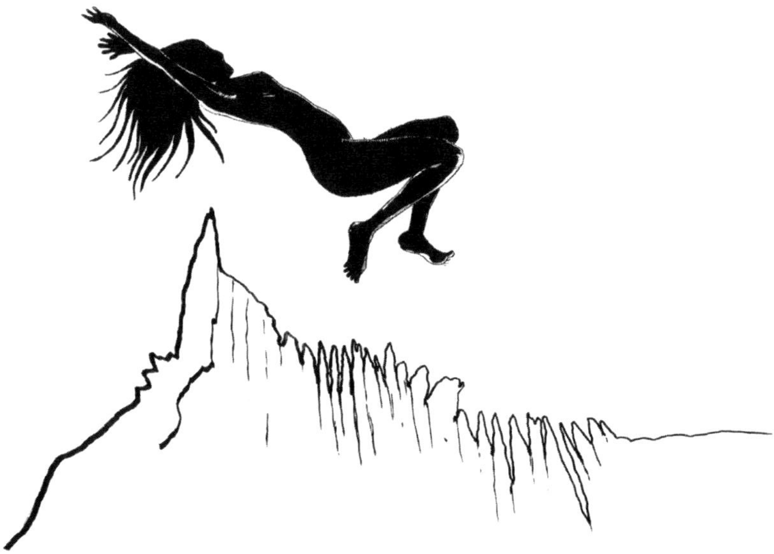

to her father that Timpanac was not only her choice but also the right young brave for her?

Her father came up with an idea that would pit the young braves against each other. It was a contest of bravery, determination and skill, and whoever came out on top would win the young maiden's hand in marriage. Ucanogos didn't like that her affection should be rewarded to just any winner when her heart beat only for Timpanac, but she knew that he was young and strong and had the best chance of beating his opponents.

The men were to kill an animal with their bare hands, race around a lake and climb to the top of a mountain peak. Easy for Timpanac, who proved himself true in every contest until the very last. While atop the mountain in his last contested battle for his future bride, his competitors, not happy with the potential outcome, wrestled Timpanac to the ground. As strong as he was, he could not fight them all. They overtook him and threw him off a cliff.

When word reached Ucanogos that her Timpanac had been killed, she was so distraught that she climbed the mountain herself and leaped to her death to join him in eternity, their two hearts finally and forever together—both in the eternal worlds and in a large cave in the very mountain where it was said the Indian maiden and her brave had died.

Tales of Strange Love

There are several versions to this Indian tale—at least twelve recorded variations, according to the National Park Service—but all have the same ending: the two lovers die and their spirits unite in death, their hearts melding together as a heart-shaped stalactite inside Utah's most popular cave. If you've ever visited the caves of Mountain Timpanogos, managed by the NPS, you may have seen the heart-shaped stalactite. The next time you visit, maybe this story will come to mind.

Or maybe you'll recall one of the other similar stories about it. In some of the tales, Ucanogos is named Utahna and Timpanac is Timpanogos—not a brave at all but a sort of Indian god. The myriad stories also make it tough to know from whence came the mountain's name. Was it named after the two lovers, in memory of Timpanogos himself or the Timpanogots Ute Tribe? Still, some believe the stories started with Eugene Lusk "Timp" Roberts, a professor at Brigham Young University who in the early 1900s made up the original tale in an effort to promote the mountain as a tourist destination.

Perhaps we'll never know the truth, although it has been said that even folktales are based on some fact. What we do know is that there is a heart-shaped stalactite inside one of the mountain's caves. It is an interesting study in geology. The mountain—which stretches through Provo, Orem, Pleasant Grove and American Fork—includes three natural caves that contain at least forty-two types of differing rock formations.

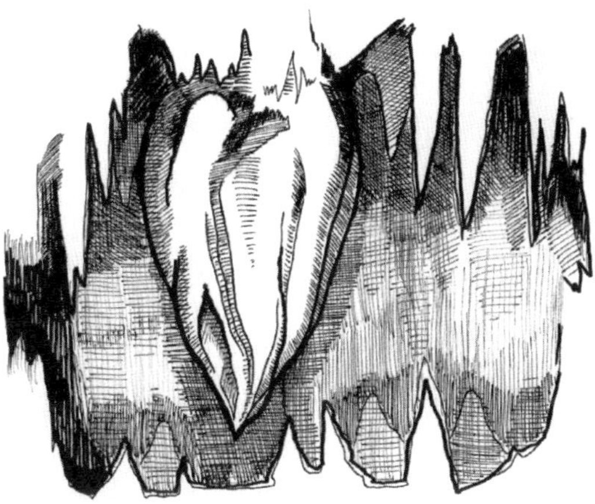

BANISHED

What do you get when you cross an outlaw, a grave robber and a ghost? The answer is the Legend of John Baptiste, one of the more colorful and interesting tales of old Utah. I shared this story in my book *Haunted Utah*, but it seems fitting to also share the tale here. For our purposes, the story begins with a man named Moroni Clawson. He may have had the name of a Book of Mormon prophet, but Clawson was no saint. He was instead one of several men accused of robbing a stagecoach in December 1861, an incident in which Governor John W. Dawson was also assaulted. But you don't assault a governor without facing the consequences. Dawson was quick to seek justice, and on January 22, 1862, the *Deseret News* published his account of the incident:

> *Sir, I deem it an act of justice to make a plain statement of the circumstances connected with the brutal and unprovoked attack made on me at Mountain Dell, Ephraim Hanks' mail station, on the night of the 31st ultimo....I suspected nothing wrong until I had got nearly out of town, when Ephraim Hanks rode up and said that there were some desperate men in the city who it was possible might follow me for violence or plunder, but he rather thought not. I then asked him to go with me to his station as his appearance there would insure immunity from assault, should any be intended; but he said it was impossible for him to go, but he would go back and send Moroni Clawson, who would do just as well as he would.*

Clawson, however, wound up being "the traitor" who acted as a friend but had set him up for the attack, Dawson explained. It apparently wasn't the gang's first offense, for the governor said the "desperadoes" had "cast another stain on the city, as they have heretofore often done." Dawson ended his letter by asking for a "speedy trial and condign punishment." Some of the robbers, such as Clawson, never saw the inside of a courtroom. Instead, Clawson was shot near present-day Second South in Salt Lake City while trying to flee from law officers. He and two others were buried at the Salt Lake Cemetery. This is where things become interesting.

When Clawson's brother, George Clawson, arrived in Salt Lake to claim the body of his dead brother, he found the deceased in a "grave" condition inside the coffin. When the grave was exhumed on January 27, George was shocked to find the naked body of his brother lying facedown in the coffin.

He was saddened by the sight but also furious. Why had his brother been buried in such an irreverent manner?

As he would find out, that claim went to a city-employed gravedigger named John Baptiste. The charges came after a declothed corpse was found lying in a cemetery bush—lo and behold, there was Baptiste pushing a wheelbarrow full of clothes.

George Clawson and "three or four other men" searched Baptiste's house while the gravedigger was away, although his wife was home, and soon found enough evidence—dead men's clothes—to convict the gravedigger of grave robbing. Officials believed that the clothing and jewelry had been stolen from at least 350 bodies he had interred. Families were hurt and angered at the ghoulish activity of Baptiste, who was described by one newspaper writer as "entirely conscienceless."

The other interesting part of this story is what allegedly happened to Baptiste after his conviction. According to the story, Brigham Young said that if it were left up to him, he would "make him a fugitive and vagabond upon the earth." The idea was hatched: Baptiste was to be banished to Freemont Island in the Great Salt Lake.

If there was anywhere as isolated in 1860s Utah, it wasn't known. After providing Baptiste with shelter and provisions, law officers left him alone on the island. They returned several weeks later with more food and found the former gravedigger "getting along very well in his loneliness." Satisfied, the officers left, but when they again returned to the island a few weeks later, they didn't find any trace of Baptiste or any clues to what may have happened to him.

The *Deseret Weekly* was of the opinion that one of two things happened: "either that he perished in the Lake in attempting to reach the mainland, or that he really succeeded," reads the June 3, 1893 article. "That he died on the island is wholly disbelieved, because during the years that have elapsed since, every foot of it has been traversed at least a score, perhaps a hundred times, by sheepmen and cattlemen, and no trace of his remains has ever been found." The same article noted that some people believed that Baptiste made his way to Promontory and on to Montana, where later it was allegedly reported he was seen working the mines; others believed he joined an emigrant party and headed to San Francisco and then to Southern California, where he died.

Whatever happened to Baptiste—or however much of the story is true—it sparked one of Utah's more interesting ghost tales. It's been said that the ghost of the gravedigger turned grave robber has been seen on the shores of the Great Salt Lake carrying something in his arms. If you're lucky enough to catch a glimpse of this lonely spirit, you might notice that he is holding a bundle of clothes, dirty and wet. Like the mystery of his death, it is not clear if they are his or from one of his interred victims.

Strangers at the Ranch

The Uinta Basin is ruggedly scenic country, where thick forests and jagged mountains give color and ambience to the expansive region in northeastern Utah. The people in nearby communities such as Roosevelt or Vernal are friendly, but some of them may flit their eyes with suspicion when they notice a stranger has come to town. Most places have their mysteries, and the basin's has to do with a secretive ranch that has been made popular in paranormal circles. It's called Skinwalker Ranch, but it is sometimes referred to as "UFO Ranch" because of the many alleged unexplained sightings that have occurred here.

Stories about the ranch, which sits near an Indian reservation in the expansive rough of nature south of Fort Duchesne, stretch back many years. Local Indians believe that the area is haunted by shape-shifting creatures the Ute and Navajo tribes call "skinwalkers." According to the legend, skinwalkers are able to pass between dimensions, often haunting our world with their otherworldly presence. Bigfoot-like creatures, flying orbs, fierce animals with red eyes and bullet-proof skin and poltergeist activity are just some of the things reported at the ranch.

The stories were made popular after George A. Knapp produced a series of articles about the ranch for the now-defunct *Las Vegas Mercury*. He later coauthored a book with Colm A. Kelleher titled *Hunt for the Skinwalker: Science Confronts the Unexplained at a Remote Ranch in Utah*, which tells of the strange goings-on that Tom and Ellen Gorman experienced when they lived at the ranch in the 1980s. Among their encounters with the unexplained, the Gormans said that they often saw hovering triangular craft floating over fields and wolflike creatures with piercing red eyes. In their book, the authors claimed that the property was acquired by the National Institute for Discovery and Science to study anecdotal reports of UFOs and paranormal activity, and that during their stay at the ranch they investigated nearly one hundred evidences of unexplained phenomena.

Terry and Gwen Sherman, who lived at the ranch before selling it to the NIDS in the 1990s, told the *Deseret News* in a June 30, 1996 article that they were privy to repeated UFO sightings in a period of just fifteen months—"a small boxlike craft with a white light, a 40-foot-long object and a huge ship the size of several football fields," the article reads. "They've seen one craft emit a wavy red ray or light beam as it flies along. They've seen other airborne lights, some of which have emerged from orange, circular doorways that seem to appear in midair. They've videotaped two of the sightings." The family claimed that they found strange craft imprints in their fields and mutilated cows on their property, heard unfamiliar voices above them and were even followed in their vehicle by a strange light.

The story of Skinwalker Ranch is a popular one in Utah, so why is it included in a book of forgotten tales? Because the mystery of the site continues to deepen instead of come to light, and it seems that no matter how much you hear about the strange goings-on at the ranch, if you revisit the topic at a later date there are stories you didn't hear about the last time you checked. At least that seems to have been the case with my research. What the truth is behind the tales is still open for debate, but alleged sightings

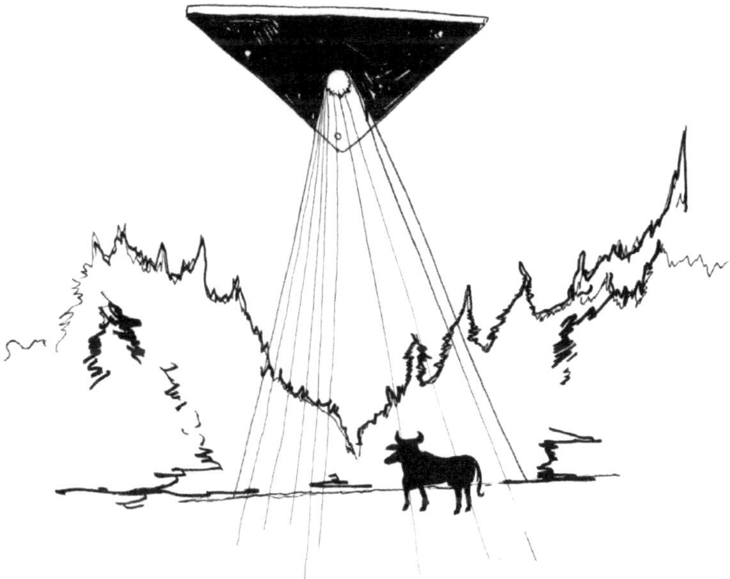

of UFOs and other unexplained phenomena have been going on for a long time in the Uinta Basin.

Stories about UFOs have circulated in the basin since at least the 1950s. By some estimates, according to the authors, more than half of the basin's residents have seen anomalous objects in the sky. During the 1960s and '70s, the Utah Highway Patrol received so many reports about UFO sightings that the department stopped following up on them. Junior Hicks, a local UFO historian, collected more than four hundred stories of UFO sightings that had occurred in the basin. Hicks even shared a personal experience that occurred in the '70s when he "watched an orange ball fly over the town of Roosevelt at a high rate of speed, then make an abrupt right-angle turn. The ball hovered in the air over the town before zipping out of sight at an incredible speed. In at least six of the cases he investigated, witnesses say they saw not only the spaceships but also the occupants of the craft." One rancher described a ship's occupants as "wearing white coveralls."

If these stories are true, what is it about the Uinta Basin that sparks such strange, sometimes frightening experiences? If there are such things as otherworldly beings, what interest do they have in a small ranch in rural Utah? Some believe the stories are exaggerated, that such things as cattle mutilations and crop circles are easily explained as the work of pranksters; others believe that the ranch is a government site used for secret military purposes. But like all good mysteries, the answers don't come easily. The adventure is in the investigation.

As someone who is at least somewhat familiar with the basin, having spent much of my youth in its quiet communities, I acknowledge that stories of the strange and otherworldly at least at one time were readily shared and talked about. Growing up and visiting my grandparents in a small town in Duchesne County, I remember hearing stories about Bigfoot, the Moon Lake Monster and creepy UFO sightings. I went to bed one night and woke to my own encounter with the unexplained. I wrote of the experience several years ago, but this is the first time it has been published. This is that story.

A Personal Experience in the Uinta Basin

I have fond childhood memories of time spent in the Uinta Basin. It is where my father was raised with his five siblings. Later, as a young married man, he moved with his new bride to Southern California, where the jobs were better and where my three siblings and I were born. Almost every summer, though, we'd pack up and head to Utah and my father's old stomping grounds in the Uinta Basin.

There was always something special about visiting Grandma and Grandpa's house, which stood on tree-lined property off a roadway in rural Altonah. Behind the house were an old chicken coop, garage and Grandma Mae's famous Pump House, where she stored all kinds of foodstuffs and treats. Farther back were hay fields, abandoned barns and a clear, cold-water stream that ran in the shade of tall poplar trees.

Except for the occasional moo of a cow, song of a meadowlark or clapping of tree leaves as a gentle breeze pushed against them (or the even rarer occasion of a car passing along the roadway), the place was quiet—sometimes too quiet.

Voices inside the house, however, let me know that life was good, and I remember sitting in the cozy living room, Grandpa in his own special chair, listening to my parents and grandparents talk about times past and present. It was always a pleasant, peaceful experience for me to visit Dad's childhood home—except for that one night when I heard loud, heavy footsteps beneath the window where I lay in bed, trying to fall asleep.

The bedroom I was occupying was on the second story, its window facing the rural roadway and the expansive farmland beyond. Across the street was a dilapidated barn—only later did I learn from my mother that it once was used as a dance hall. Heavy quilt blankets were pulled up to my chin as I lay in bed trying to fall asleep, wondering what the grownups were talking about downstairs. And then I heard a noise, like the sound of heavy footsteps, along with the crunch of fallen leaves that carpeted the lawn outside. My young child's mind turned to images of Sasquatch, of whom I'd heard stories in the basin. The footsteps grew louder, heavier, as they came closer to my window. I called for my mom.

"I heard footsteps," I said. "There's something outside." The sound stopped. Was someone standing just below my window? We looked out the window, but it was too dark to see much of anything.

"I don't feel good," I said, a wave of nausea overcoming me. I padded downstairs to the bathroom, where I threw up that night's dinner. I had felt fine going to bed and only became ill after I heard the footsteps. Thinking back on the experience, my sick tummy probably was caused by fear of what I imagined was outside my bedroom window. Dad was up talking with his parents, and after I had finished in the bathroom, my mom told him what I had heard. Grandpa said it probably was only a cow that had wandered out of a nearby field. To prove his point, he and Dad went outside to check the yard. They returned a few minutes later and said they didn't find a cow, horse or anything else. No fences were broken. No traces of footprints—human, cow or otherwise—were found the next morning.

To this day, I do not know what caused the noise I heard outside my bedroom window. I only know that I did hear those heavy footsteps. I like to assume it was only a farm animal that snuck away before Dad and Grandpa could find it, leaving no trace of its visit behind, although I recall it not sounding like how a four-legged animal would walk. And interestingly, I was the only person in the house who had heard any footsteps at all, which is odd in itself. The grownups were in the living room, which was beneath my bedroom, and both the living room and bedroom windows faced the same direction. If something had been outside my window, it also would have been outside the living room window. But the grownups said they never heard anything like what I had heard.

What was it that I heard? Where did it go? And why was I the only one to hear it? Was the presence, whatever it was, of the Skinwalker variety—there one moment and gone the next? I've chalked it up to another unexplained mystery in the Uinta Basin. But I've wondered since then why some people are more prone to supernatural activity than others. Why do some people visit alleged haunted sites, for instance, or lie sleepless in bed and claim to have weird experiences, while others have very ordinary experiences? I don't know the answer to that. Perhaps you do.

Bibliography

Arave, Lynn. "Does Bigfoot Roam while Gold Lies Hidden Under Indian Maiden?" *Deseret News*, September 30, 2003.

———. "Mythical Beasts Lurk in 5 Utah Lakes." *Deseret News*, September 23, 2001.

Bagley, Pat. "Living History: Mark Twain Was 'Rough It' When He Met Brigham Young." *Salt Lake Tribune*, January 5, 2013. http://archive.sltrib.com/story.php?ref=/sltrib/news/55570819-78/twain-salt-lake-brigham.html.csp.

Bagley, Will. *Blood of the Prophets: Brigham Young and the Massacre at Mountain Meadows*. Norman: University of Oklahoma Press, 2002.

Bennion, Sherilyn Cox. "Journalism in Utah." Utah Education Network. http://www.uen.org/utah_history_encyclopedia/j/JOURNALISM.html.

Benson, Lee. "About Utah: Story of First KFC Shows Anything Can Happen." *Deseret News*, January 19, 2012. Retrieved from http://www.deseretnews.com/article/700217162/Story-of-first-KFC-shows-anything-can-happen.html?pg=all.

Biography.com. "Famous People Born in Utah." http://www.biography.com/people/groups/born-in-utah.

Black, Susan Easton, and Larry C. Porter, eds. *Lion of the Lord: Essays on the Life & Service of Brigham Young*. Salt Lake City, UT: Deseret Book, 1995.

Boren, Kerry Ross, and Lisa Lee Boren. *The Gold of Carre-Shinob: The Final Chapter in the Mystery of the Lost Rhoades Mines, Seven Lost Cities, and Montezuma's Treasure*. Springville, UT: Cedar Fort, 1998.

Butters, Whitney. "Capitol Theatre Serves as a 'Memory Builder' 101 Years After Its Construction." *Deseret News*, August 23, 2014. Retrieved from http://www.deseretnews.com/article/865609372/Capitol-Theatre-serves-as-a-memory-builder-101-years-after-its-construction.html.

Canhan, Matt. "Mormon Populace Picks Up the Pace in Utah." *Salt Lake Tribune*, November 30, 2014. http://www.sltrib.com/news/1842825-155/mormon-populace-picks-up-the-pace.

Cannon, George Q., ed. *Journal of Discourses.* 26 vols. Liverpool, UK: Latter-day Saints' Book Depot, 1861.

———. "The Logan Temple." *Millennial Star*, November 12, 1877, 743.

Capitol Reef County. "History: The Wolverton Mill—Hanskville, Utah." http://www.capitolreef.org/history.html.

Carter, D. Robert. "Josie Bassett—Jensen's Remarkable Woman Rancher." Utah History to Go. http://historytogo.utah.gov/utah_chapters/pioneers_and_cowboys/josiebassett.html.

Centers for Disease Control and Prevention. "Rocky Mountain Spotted Fever." http://www.cdc.gov/rmsf.

Christensen, Douglas K. "Moroni's 36 Year Trek to New York." Book of Mormon Archaeological Forum. http://www.bmaf.org/articles/joseph_rocky_mountains__christensen.

The Church of Jesus Christ of Latter-day Saints. *Hymns.* Salt Lake City, UT: 1985.

———. "The Manifesto and the End of Plural Marriage." https://www.lds.org/topics/the-manifesto-and-the-end-of-plural-marriage?lang=eng.

———. *Mountain of the Lord.* Video. Salt Lake City, UT: self-published, 1993.

———. "Plural Marriage in Kirtland and Nauvoo." https://www.lds.org/topics/plural-marriage-in-kirtland-and-nauvoo?lang=eng&old=true.

———. *Presidents of the Church Student Manual.* Salt Lake City, UT: self-published, 2012.

———. *Primary 5: Doctrine and Covenants and Church History.* Salt Lake City, UT: self-published, 1997.

———. *Teachings of Presidents of the Church: Brigham Young.* Salt Lake City, UT: self-published, 1997.

Denton, Sally. *American Massacre: The Tragedy at Mountain Meadows, September 1857.* New York: Vintage Books, 2003.

Deseret News. "Governor Dawson's Statement." January 22, 1862.

Deseret Weekly. "Baptiste's Banishment." June 3, 1893.

DeVoy, Beverly. "Monster or Mere Mirage?" *Deseret News*, March 18, 1991. Retrieved from http://www.deseretnews.com/article/152180/MONSTER-OR-MERE-MIRAGE.html.

Doctrine and Covenants Student Manual. "Section 129: Keys for Determining If Administrations Are from God." Salt Lake City, UT: Church of Jesus Christ of Latter-day Saints, 2002. Retrieved from https://www.lds.org/manual/doctrine-and-covenants-student-manual/sections-122-131/section-129-keys-for-determining-if-administrations-are-from-god?lang=eng.

Dunn, Loren C. "The Temple Is the Heart of Sacred Work." *Church News*, February 6, 1993. Retrieved from http://www.ldschurchnewsarchive.com/articles/print/23782/The-temple-is-the-heart-of-sacred-work.html.

Effective Language Learning. "English Language." http://www.effectivelanguagelearning.com/language-guide/english-language.

Ensign. "The Manti Temple" (October 1978). The Church of Jesus Christ of Latter-day Saints. Retrieved from https://www.lds.org/ensign/1978/03/the-manti-temple?lang=eng.

Gaunt, LaRene. "The Power of God Was with Us." *Ensign* (March 1993). Retrieved from https://www.lds.org/ensign/1993/03/the-power-of-god-was-with-us?lang=eng.

Gibbons, Francis. *Wilford Woodruff: Wondrous Worker, Prophet of God*. Salt Lake City, UT: Deseret Book Company, 1988.

Gordon, Kathryn Jenkins. *Colorful Characters in Mormon History: The Good, the Bad, and the Hilarious!* American Fork, UT: Covenant Communications Inc., 2015.

Hancock, Laura. "Census Bureau Shows Number of Blacks in Utah Up 7.2% in a Year." *Deseret News*, June 10, 2010. See also United States Census Bureau. "QuickFacts: Utah." https://www.census.gov/quickfacts/table/PST045215/49,00.

History.com. "This Day in History: July 29, 1776—Escalante and Dominguez Begin Expedition." http://www.history.com/this-day-in-history/escalante-and-dominguez-begin-expedition.

Holzapfel, Richard Neitzel, and Christopher C. Jones. "'John the Revelator': The Written Revelations of John Taylor." BYU Studies Center. Retrieved from https://rsc.byu.edu/archived/champion-liberty-john-taylor/john-revelator-written-revelations-john-taylor.

Horne, Dennis B. *Latter Leaves in the Life of Lorenzo Snow*. Springville, UT: Cedar Fort Inc., 2012.

Hurst, Winston. "Anasazi." Utah History Encyclopedia, Utah History to Go. http://historytogo.utah.gov/utah_chapters/american_indians/anasazi.html.

I Know that My Redeemer Lives: Latter-day Prophets Testify of the Savior. Salt Lake City, UT: Deseret Book Company, 1990.

Journal of Discourses. 26 vols. London: Latter-day Saints Book Depot, 1854.

Kelleher, Colm A., and George Knapp. *Hunt for the Skinwalker: Science Confronts the Unexplained at a Remote Ranch in Utah.* New York: Paraview Pocket Books, 2005.

Law, Steven. "Butch Cassidy and the Sundance Kid Didn't Die in a Bolivian Gunfight." KSL News, September 12, 2011. https://www.ksl.com/?sid=17130775.

Lee, John D. *Mormonism Unveiled: The Life and Confession of John D. Lee and the Complete Life of Brigham Young.* Albuquerque: University of New Mexico Press, 2008.

Legends of America. "Utah Legends: Bear Lake Sea Monster." http://www.legendsofamerica.com/ut-bearlakemonster.html.

Lyman-Whitney, Susan. "Little-Known Facts About Women in American History." *Deseret News*, March 12, 1995. http://www.deseretnews.com/article/409243/LITTLE-KNOWN-FACTS-ABOUT-WOMEN-IN-AMERICAN-HISTORY.html?pg=all.

McCullough, David. *1776.* New York: Simon & Schuster, 2005.

Monson, Samuel C. "Deseret Alphabet." Encyclopedia of Mormonism, found at BYU Harold B. Lee Library. http://eom.byu.edu/index.php/Deseret_Alphabet.

Moore, Carrie A. "Church Issues Apology for Massacre." *Deseret News*, September 11, 2007. Retrieved from http://www.deseretnews.com/article/695209108/Church-issues-apology-for-massacre.html?pg=all.

Moore, Richard G. "The Deseret Alphabet Experiment." BYU Religious Studies Center. https://rsc.byu.edu/archived/volume-7-number-3-2006/deseret-alphabet-experiment.

Moroni's Latter-day Saint Page. "Lorenzo Snow Sees Jesus Christ in the Salt Lake Temple." http://www.moroni10.com/mormon_history/lorenzo-snow-jesus-temple.html.

Mountain Meadows Association. http://www.mtn-meadows-assoc.com.

Murphy, Miram B. "African Americans Built Churches." History Blazer, July 1996, as found on Utah History to Go. http://historytogo.utah.gov/people/ethnic_cultures/africanamericansbuiltchurches.html.

National Park Service. "The 1846 Trek." https://www.nps.gov/mopi/learn/historyculture/history1.htm.

———. "Josie Basset Morris." https://www.nps.gov/dino/learn/historyculture/josiebassettmorris.htm.

———. "The Legend of Mount Timpanogos." https://www.nps.gov/tica/learn/historyculture/the-legend-of-timpanogos.htm.

———. "Newspaper Rock." https://www.nps.gov/pefo/learn/historyculture/newspaper-rock.htm.

———. "Viewing Petroglyphs and Pictographs." Dinosaur National Monument. https://www.nps.gov/dino/learn/historyculture/viewing-petroglyphs-and-pictographs.htm.

Nix, Elizabeth. "6 Things You Might Not Know About Butch Cassidy." History.com. http://www.history.com/news/history-lists/6-things-you-might-not-know-about-butch-cassidy.

Olsen, Nolan P. *The Logan Temple: The First 100 Years*. N.p., 1978.

Oxford Royale Academy. "Why Is English So Hard to Learn?" https://www.oxford-royale.co.uk/articles/learning-english-hard.html.

Packer, Boyd K. "The Holy Temple." *Ensign* (October 2010). Retrieved from https://www.lds.org/ensign/2010/10/the-holy-temple?lang=eng.

PBS. "John Doyle Lee (1812–1877)." New Perspectives on the West. http://www.pbs.org/weta/thewest/people/i_r/lee.htm.

———. "The Last Words of John D. Lee Spoken at His Execution for the Mountain Meadows Massacre, March 23, 1877." New Perspectives on the West. http://www.pbs.org/weta/thewest/resources/archives/six/lee.htm.

Peterson, H. Donl. "Moroni, the Last of the Nephite Prophets." BYU Religious Studies Center. https://rsc.byu.edu/archived/book-mormon-fourth-nephi-through-moroni-zion-destruction/18-moroni-last-nephite-prophets.

———. *Moroni: Ancient Prophet, Modern Messenger*. Springville, UT: Cedar Fort Inc., 2008.

Peterson, John A. "Living History: Utah's Black Hawk War Was the Longest, Costliest and Bloodiest in State History." *Salt Lake Tribune*, September 2, 2011. http://archive.sltrib.com/story.php?ref=/sltrib/news/52507608-78/utah-indians-black-hawk.html.csp.

Pierce, Scott D. "Investigating Salt Lake City's 'Haunted' Capitol Theatre." *Salt Lake Tribune*, August 21, 2012. Retrieved from http://archive.sltrib.com/story.php?ref=/sltrib/entertainment/54717615-81/theatre-capitol-lake-salt.html.csp.

Priesthood. Salt Lake City, UT: Deseret Book Company, 1981.

Primary 5: Doctrine and Covenants and Church History. "Lesson 38: Brigham Young Leads the Church" (1997): 216–21. The Church of Jesus Christ of Latter-day Saints. https://www.lds.org/manual/primary-5-doctrine-and-covenants-and-church-history/lesson-38-brigham-young-leads-the-church?lang=eng.

Public Broadcasting Service. "New Perspectives on the West: John Doyle Lee (1812–1877)." http://www.pbs.org/weta/thewest/people/i_r/lee.htm.

Rees, Catherine. "You May Be Surprised to Learn that These 20 Famous People Are from Utah." Only in Your State, July 25, 2015. http://www.onlyinyourstate.com/utah/famous-people-from-ut.

Roberts, David. "Riddles of the Anasazi: What Awful Event Forced the Anasazi to Flee Their Homeland, Never to Return." *Smithsonian Magazine* (July 2003). http://www.smithsonianmag.com/people-places/riddles-of-the-anasazi-85274508/?no-ist.

Rolly, Paul. "Rolly: Mormon Group Gets Lesson on Black History in Utah—From Celebrated Soldiers to Jane Manning James and Elijah Abel." *Salt Lake Tribune*, June 9, 2016. http://www.sltrib.com/home/3988109-155/rolly-mormon-group-gets-lesson-on.

Salt Lake Temple. "Dedication Prayer." http://www.ldschurchtemples.com/saltlake/prayer.

Schindler, Hal. "Early Tribune, Deseret News Made Trash Talk an Art Form—Tribune, Deseret News Took Off Gloves." *Salt Lake Tribune*, April 14, 1996, found on Utah Division of State History. https://heritage.utah.gov/tag/early-tribune-deseret-news-made-trash-talk-an-art-form-tribune-deseret-news-took-off-gloves.

Smart, Christopher. "Forgotten Non-Mormon Utah Leader Finally Gets a Headstone." *Salt Lake Tribune*, June 16, 2014. http://archive.sltrib.com/story.php?ref=/sltrib/news/58060750-78/baskin-utah-lake-history.html.csp.

Smith, Paul Thomas. *Prophetic Destiny: The Saints in the Rocky Mountains*. Salt Lake City, UT: Covenant Communications Inc., 1996.

Snow, LeRoi C. "An Experience of My Father's." *Improvement Era*, September 1933, 677.

Staker, Susan, ed. *Waiting for World's End: The Diaries of Wilford Woodruff*. Salt Lake City, UT: Signature Books, 1993.

Stone, Eileen Hallet. "Living History: Robert Newton Baskin Fought Utah's Fusion of Church and State." *Salt Lake Tribune*, May 23, 2014. http://archive.sltrib.com/story.php?ref=/sltrib/mobile3/57981687-219/baskin-utah-lake-mormon.html.csp.

Stuy, Brian H. "'Come, Let Us Go Up to the Mountain of the Lord': The Salt Lake Temple Dedication." *Dialogue* 31, no. 3. https://www.dialoguejournal.com/wp-content/uploads/sbi/articles/Dialogue_V31N03_115.pdf.

Sullivan, Marlene Bateman. "'Friend and Brother': Jacob Hamblin, Man of Peace." *Ensign* (October 1984). https://www.lds.org/ensign/1984/10/friend-and-brother-jacob-hamblin-man-of-peace?lang=eng.

Thompson, Bonnie. *Folklore in the Bear Lake Valley*. Salt Lake City, UT: Granite Publishing, 1972.

Twain, Mark. *Roughing It*. Chicago: Sun-Times Media Group, 1872.

Utah.com. "Jacob Hamblin Home." https://utah.com/mormon/hamblin-home.

Vaifanua, Tamara. "Forgotten Central Utah Massacre of Paiute Indians Remembered 150 Years Later." Fox13, April 19, 2016. Retrieved from http://fox13now.com/2016/04/19/forgotten-central-utah-massacre-of-paiute-indians-remembered-150-years-later.

Van Eyck, Zack. "Frequent Fliers." *Deseret News*, June 30, 1996. Retrieved from http://www.deseretnews.com/article/498676/FREQUENT-FLIERS.html.

Van Leer, Twila. "The Lost Rhoads Mine." *Deseret News*, July 2, 1996.

Van Orden, Bruce A. "Loyal Friend of the Book of Mormon." *Ensign* (August 1986). Retrieved from https://www.lds.org/ensign/1986/08/george-reynolds-loyal-friend-of-the-book-of-mormon?lang=eng.

———. *Prisoner for Conscience' Sake: The Life of George C. Reynolds.* Salt Lake City, UT: Deseret Book Company, 1992.

Visit Utah. "Utah History Past." http://www.visitutah.com/utah-history-past.

Walker, Neil Alexander. "A Complete Guide to Reading and Writing the Deseret Alphabet." University of California–Los Angeles, Department of Chemistry and Biology. http://copper.chem.ucla.edu/~jericks/Historical%20or%20Technical/Linguistics/Deseret_Guide.pdf.

Water History. "The Wolverton Mill." Bureau of Land Management, Hanksville Utah. http://www.waterhistory.org/histories/wolverton/wolverton.pdf.

Weeks, Andy. *Haunted Utah: Ghosts and Strange Phenomena of the Beehive State.* Mechanicsburg, PA: Stackpole Books, 2012.

———. *A History of Mormon Landmarks in Utah: Monuments of Faith.* Charleston, SC: The History Press, 2015.

———. "3rd Annual Paddlefest Brings Fun and Adventure." *Vernal Express*, June 23, 2015. UBMedia. http://www.ubmedia.biz/vernal/expressions/article_23a7d00e-19ce-11e5-a82e-c3e02e9c4f71.html.

Weeks, Dora Mae. *Sacred Memories of Dora Mae MacAfee Weeks*. N.p.: self-published, 2004.

Wood, Benjamin. "'Forgotten' Massacre of Utah Paiute Group Recalled with New Monument." *Salt Lake Tribune*, April 22, 2016. Retrieved from http://www.sltrib.com/home/3808340-155/forgotten-massacre-of-innocent-utah-paiute.

Woodruff, Wilford. "A Vision, Salt Lake City, Night of Dec 16, 1877." Journal entry, presumably a vision of John Taylor, dated June 15, 1878. As quoted in "John Taylor's Last Days Vision." Latter-day Conservative. http://www.latterdayconservative.com/john-taylor/john-taylors-last-days-vision.

About the Author

Andy Weeks is an award-winning journalist and author of several regional books on travel and history, including two other volumes on the Beehive State, *A History of Mormon Landmarks in Utah* and *Haunted Utah*.